Ethics and

United States Foreign Policy

ETHICS
AND
UNITED
STATES
FOREIGN
POLICY

by ERNEST W. LEFEVER

LIVING AGE BOOKS

published by MERIDIAN BOOKS, INC. *New York* 1957

Ernest W. Lefever

Ernest W. Lefever is a research analyst in foreign affairs with the Legislative Reference Service of the Library of Congress. He received his bachelor's degree at Elizabethtown College, and his B.D. and Ph. D. degrees from Yale University. An ordained Protestant clergyman, Dr. Lefever has taught political science at the University of Maryland and social ethics at Westminster Theological Seminary in Maryland. Dr. Lefever has served as an international affairs specialist with the National Council of the Churches of Christ in the United States. He spent the first three years after World War II in Europe as a field secretary of the World's Alliance of YMCA's. He has traveled extensively in Europe and Asia in other educational capacities. On a grant from the Rockefeller Foundation, Dr. Lefever did research in ethics and foreign policy at the School of Advanced International Studies, Johns Hopkins University. He has been a foreign correspondent in Germany for *The Christian Century* and Religious News Service, and has written for many religious periodicals.

A Living Age Books Original Edition
First published by Meridian Books, Inc. October 1957
First printing September 1957

To Margaret

CONTENTS

PREFACE

Barbara Ward recently referred to United States foreign policy as "everybody's destiny." Allowing for an
understandable literary hyperbole, no informed and
responsible person can deny the essential truth of her
statement nor escape the moral implications of this
truth. The American people have a moral responsibility for international peace and security commensurate
with the tremendous political and economic power
which history has conferred upon them.

In our tragically divided world is it possible for a
superpower like the United States to formulate and
carry out a foreign policy based upon moral principle?
Are ethics and politics two separate realms which are
joined only in the pious platitudes of preachers and
politicians and never in the real world of political decision? Can the principles of Western morality contribute to the understanding of international politics and
foreign policy?

To deal with these questions of politics and ethics I
found it necessary to combine fact, analysis and evalu-

ation. I have attempted to include in this book those facts and events about United States foreign relations, especially since the end of World War II, which are essential to any sound understanding of our Government's response to the problems and vicissitudes of world politics. These facts are presented in the context of a political analysis which owes much to the thought of Reinhold Niebuhr, Hans J. Morgenthau, William T. R. Fox, Walter Lippmann, George F. Kennan and Kenneth W. Thompson.

This book attempts to relate the insights and affirmations of Judaeo-Christian ethics to the problems and direction of United States foreign policy. My normative point of reference is rooted in the Judaeo-Christian tradition. Although I am a Protestant I have attempted to draw mainly upon those great affirmations about the nature of man and of history which are common to the central traditions of Judaism, Roman Catholicism and Protestantism and which provide the foundations of Western morality.

This book is a sympathetic but critical interpretation of the major direction of United States foreign policy since 1945. My presentation of fact, analysis and judgment is based upon what might be called a morally responsible and politically realistic theory of international politics. Consequently I have attempted to relate the descriptive facts and analytical insights of political science to the normative judgments of religious ethics. It is difficult to combine description with analysis, analysis with judgment and judgment with advocacy, but I hope the reader can ascertain without too much difficulty where fact left off and evaluation began.

I am deeply indebted to A. William Loos, Executive Director of The Church Peace Union, who commissioned me to write this manuscript and who saw the project through from its original conception as a brief pamphlet-size primer to the present volume. His advice and support have been invaluable. The first draft was written during 1955-1956 at the School of Advanced International Studies of Johns Hopkins University in Washington, D.C., where I was engaged in a year of research made possible by a Rockefeller Foundation grant. I am indebted both to the Rockefeller Foundation and to the School of Advanced International Studies. I wish to express my special gratitude to Paul H. Nitze, who served as my adviser at the School. I hope some of his wisdom has spilled over into this volume.

A debt of gratitude is due a number of political scientists and theologians whose sympathetic appraisal of the original manuscript encouraged me to transform the primer-like first draft into a larger and less superficial book. Among those who made helpful suggestions were Professor Reinhold Niebuhr of Union Theological Seminary, Professor Hans J. Morgenthau of the University of Chicago, Professor Amry Vandenbosch of the University of Kentucky, Professor Creighton Lacy of the Duke University Divinity School and Professor Alexander Miller of Stanford University. I also received valuable criticism from the Rev. Mr. Herman F. Reissig of the Congregational Christian Council for Social Action and Mr. Edward L. Nestingen, program secretary of the National Student Council of the Y.M.C.A.

I am indebted also to Professor Elmer Plischke and Professor Franklin L. Burdette of the University of Maryland who made helpful suggestions for improving chapters three and six respectively, and to Professor Robert Tufts of Oberlin College for his criticism of chapter five.

Mr. Arthur A. Cohen, director of Meridian Books, deserves a special note of gratitude for his personal interest in this book, for his splendid editorial counsel and for his willingness to cooperate with The Church Peace Union in this joint enterprise. Any merit this book may have is due to many persons, acknowledged and unacknowledged, but as in any such effort what has been said and how it has been said is the final responsibility of the author alone.

E.W.L.

HYATTSVILLE, MARYLAND
August 1957

Introduction by
HANS J. MORGENTHAU

Dominant elements in Western culture, and American culture in particular, have consistently misunderstood the nature of foreign policy, and they have done so in the name of morality. In the process, our culture has deformed its understanding of morality and corrupted its moral judgment as well. It has imagined that the tension between foreign policy and morality, given in immediate experience, could easily be made to disappear in one of two ways. Either there could be a kind of reconciliation, a compromise by which foreign policy would be made moral, at least up to the point of non-violence and harmonious cooperation, and the moral law would be adapted to the exigencies of politics; perhaps there might even be two different kinds of moral law, one for man as such and as citizen of his nation and one for the relations among nations, the latter permitting what the former frowns upon. Or else men would have a choice between power politics, morally bad, and another kind of foreign policy not tainted with the lust for power. In any event, there was presumed to be a way out of the dilemma with which the demands of foreign policy appear to confront the moral conscience.

The truth is that there is no way out. The moral dilemma of foreign policy is but a special and—it is true—particularly flagrant case of the moral dilemma which faces man on all levels of social action. Man cannot help sinning when he acts in relation to his fellow-men; he may be able to minimize that sinfulness of social action, but he cannot escape it. For no social action can be completely free of the taint of egotism which, as selfishness, pride, or self-deception, seeks for the actor more than is his due. What is true of all social action is particularly true of political action and, within the latter, of foreign policy. For man's aspiration for power over other men, which is of the very essence of politics, implies the denial of what is the very core of Judaeo-Christian morality—respect for man as an end in himself. The power relation is the very denial of that respect; for it seeks to use man as means to the end of another man. This denial is particularly flagrant in foreign policy; for the civilizing influences of law, morality, and mores are less effective here than they are on the domestic political scene.

How was it possible for our culture to misunderstand this moral dilemma of foreign policy and, turning its gaze from it, try to smooth and gloss over the conflict, thus doing justice neither to the responsibilities of foreign policy nor to the majesty of the moral law? This escape from both power politics and true morality stems in the main from three factors: man's ambivalent relationship to power and morality, the illusions of nineteenth-century liberalism, and the misunderstanding of the American experience.

The objective position of man on the international scene is always and of necessity ambivalent. While he seeks power over others, others seek power over him.

His intellectual and moral attitudes toward power reflect this ambivalence of his objective position. While he takes the power drives of others for what they are or worse, he will close his eyes to his own aspirations for power, which appear to him as something different and nobler—justified by necessity and ethics—than they actually are. Thus ideological concealments, rationalizations, and justifications of necessity blind us both to the ubiquity and the moral deficiency of the aspiration for power. As John Adams put it:

> Power always thinks it has a great soul and vast views beyond the comprehension of the weak and that it is doing God's service when it is violating all His laws. Our passions, ambitions, avarice, love and resentment, etc., possess so much metaphysical subtlety and so much overpowering eloquence that they insinuate themselves into the understanding and the conscience and convert both to their party.

Two historic experiences strengthened this ideological misunderstanding and depreciation of power. One was the experience of the Victorian Age, as interpreted by liberal philosophy; the other, the experience of the first century of American history, as interpreted by a humanitarian, pacifist philosophy. To both, the struggle for power, especially on the international scene, appeared as the passing product of an ephemeral historic configuration. The liberals identified power politics with the rule of the aristocracy, an historic accident bound to disappear with the disappearance of autocratic government and its manifestations, such as trade barriers and colonialism.

The American experience seemed to provide experimental proof for the assumption that nations have a choice between power politics and a foreign policy not tainted by the lust for power. The Founding Fathers decided that the United States could not afford to get involved in the power politics of the European nations. Yet, to quote Washington, "The toils of European ambition, rivalship, interest, humor or caprice," with which the United States should have nothing to do, were the only manifestations of power politics before the eyes of America. Abstention from European power politics could, therefore, be taken to mean abstention from power politics as such. This aloofness from European power politics remained a political fact at least until the end of the nineteenth century, if not until the intervention of the United States in the First World War in 1917. While in fact this isolation was the result of a complicated interplay of political and military forces, it was interpreted primarily, if not exclusively, as the result of a deliberate choice. The United States had turned her back on power politics and was applying to her foreign relations the same humanitarian principles of human betterment and peaceful competition which had worked so well at home and had made her both unique and great as a nation among nations.

The experiences of two world wars and of the aftermath of the Second have disabused many of us of these illusions. We have learned that we cannot escape the temptation and liabilities of power politics by an act of will. We must learn to live with them and still remain civilized; that is, we must make the best of them. Yet even at best, we cannot afford to forget that they are ever with us. These historic experiences have reawakened both our understanding of politics and our moral sensibilities. We have begun to resurrect from the rubble of false philosophies which did not stand the test of experience the great perennial truths about politics and morality of which Western civilization is the record. In this task political thinkers and theologians have joined. And it reveals as much about the nature of religious thought as about politics that many of the most important modern insights about politics have come from the pens of theologians.

This book makes an important contribution to that task. It combines insight into the nature of foreign policy with awareness of the moral implications of political action. It adds another stone to that bridge of understanding which, from opposite sides of the valley, theologians and political thinkers have been building. It shows how the religiously committed and morally sensitive person can reflect on foreign policy in relevant terms. This achievement is as important for religion and morality as it is for the popular understanding of foreign policy. For it demonstrates implicitly the relevance of religion and morality, correctly understood, for politics, similarly understood.

In so doing, this book could fulfill an important practical function by exerting a beneficial effect upon the conduct of United States foreign policy. That foreign policy requires the support of public opinion, and it can only be as wise as an attentive and articulate public allows it to be. Public opinion, in order to be effective, must be articulate; it must make its voice heard, and its voice must make political sense. If the message of this book is heard and understood and put into practice, its merit will be not only intellectual and moral, but political as well.

CHAPTER ONE

America's foreign policy is everybody's destiny.
BARBARA WARD, 1956

ETHICS AND INTERNATIONAL POLITICS

If December 7, 1941, will live on in American history as a "day of infamy," November 2, 1956, may well be remembered as a day of irony. On that day our government joined with its arch enemy, the Soviet Union, and Egypt, her willing tool in the Middle East, in condemning our two closest and staunchest allies, Great Britain and France. This act, which helped to destroy the moral and political position of Britain and France in the Mediterranean world, was done in the name of morality. Herein lies its irony.

An ironic situation is a situation of incongruity in which the best efforts of men are mocked, seemingly by chance or accident. Upon closer examination, says Reinhold Niebuhr, the incongruity of irony is "discovered to be the result of more than chance." The situation is ironic, continues Niebuhr, "if virtue becomes vice through some hidden defect in the virtue; if strength becomes weakness because of the vanity to which strength may prompt the mighty man or nation; if security is transmuted into insecurity because too much reliance is placed upon it; if wisdom becomes folly because it does not know its own limits. . . . The ironic situation is distinguished . . . from tragedy by the fact that the responsibility [for it] is related to an unconscious weakness rather than to a conscious resolution." [1]

The events which led to the irony of November 2, 1956, are well known. For years there had been Arab border raids against Israel and Israeli reprisals. In November, 1954, Colonel Nasser became the strong man of Egypt. His regime was bolstered in the following year by a large shipment of heavy arms from the Soviet bloc. In December, 1955, the United States and Britain offered Nasser a program of massive aid to build the Aswan High Dam across the Nile. Nasser did not accept the aid. Instead he organized a neutralist Arab block and maneuvered to undermine the position of Britain and France in the Middle East. In June, 1956, the last British troops left the Suez Canal Zone. Five weeks later Secretary Dulles abruptly withdrew the American offer to help build the Aswan Dam. Nasser responded by promptly nationalizing the Suez Canal. Then came the long and fruitless effort of the Western powers, which depended most heavily on the Canal, to break Nasser's grip on the vital waterway. In late October, 1956, Israel, France and Britain invaded Egypt, Israel to secure her borders against further Egyptian raids and France and Britain to protect the Suez Canal and insure international control over it. On November 2 the General Assembly of the United Nations adopted by a vote of sixty-four to five an American-sponsored resolution condemning the aggression (although not actually using the word "aggression") of Israel, France and Britain, and ordering an immediate cease-fire and the withdrawal of the attacking troops. The Soviet Union joined the United States in supporting the resolution.

We have taken this position, said President Eisenhower, to "honor our pledge" to "assist the victim of aggression in the Middle East" and because "we do not accept the use of force as an instrument for the settlement of international disputes." To have taken a different position, the President declared on February 20, 1957, would have "turned back the clock of international order. . . . If the United Nations once admits that international disputes can be settled by using force, then we will have destroyed the very foundation of the organization, and the best hope of establishing a real world order. . . . Peace and justice are two sides of the same coin." Some people have found it difficult to reconcile Mr. Eisenhower's foreswearing of force in the case of the Israeli-British-French invasion of Egypt with his special message to Congress on January 5, 1957, requesting authority to employ unilaterally "the armed forces of the United States" in the Middle East, even though the President stated that our employment of force "would have to be consonant with" the Charter and recommendations of the United Nations.

For years historians, statesmen, theologians and ordinary citizens will be discussing the meaning of the events which led to and flowed from the decision of our government to abandon its friends and join its foes in one of the most serious international crises since World War II. Already interpretations vary greatly. At one extreme are President Eisenhower and Secretary Dulles, who have repeatedly justified their decision on the grounds of international morality. At the other extreme is the view of a foremost student[2] of American foreign policy who said the "first week of November, 1956, is likely to be remembered as one of the most calamitous episodes in the history of United States diplomacy."

Whatever the verdict of the future will be on America's Middle Eastern policies in 1956 and 1957, the whole chain of events dramatizes the irony of history, the almost insuperable difficulty of relating ethics to foreign policy, and the tragic consequences which often flow from a well-intentioned but simplistic reconciliation of moral principles and the ambiguities of international politics. If our "foreign policy is everybody's destiny," and if we are not the helpless pawns of a cruel and inscrutable fate, then one of the supreme tasks of our generation is to attempt to relate responsibly the moral wisdom of our Judaeo-Christian inheritance to the complex and tragic realities of world politics, and more specifically to the fateful decisions of American foreign policy.

This book is a modest attempt to deal with this problem. The writer is convinced that there is a widespread and profound confusion among religious and political leaders regarding the relation of ethics to international politics, that religion is often a source of confusion rather than understanding, and that efforts to apply morality to foreign policy frequently end in disaster. Much of this confusion flows from a misunderstanding of what international politics is on the one hand and what ethics, especially Judaeo-Christian ethics, is on the other. Many Americans do not understand the role of power in foreign policy. "Power politics" and ethics are often thought of as mutually exclusive and morally incompatible poles or political alternatives. The writer believes there is no foreign policy, however noble, which does not include "power politics," or, however cynical, which does not include moral considerations.

Nature of International Politics

World politics is a vast, unending drama. History is its stage. The actors of the present century are the governments of more than eighty legally sovereign states. Some of these nations are weak, and others are powerful. Since 1945, two of them, the United States and the Soviet Union, have been superpowers and, as such, are the chief antagonists in the global drama.

We might wish that the power and influence of the nations were more evenly distributed or that there were no superpowers or satellites, but such is not the case. The United Nations Charter affirms the "sovereign equality" of the United States, New Zealand, Ghana, Nepal and its seventy-seven other member states. But the Charter's affirmation of legal or moral equality does not alter the fact of great political and economic inequality among nations. In 1943 when the U.N. Charter was being drafted, Samuel Grafton commented: "Even after you give the squirrel a certificate which says he is quite as big as an elephant, he is still going to be smaller, and all the squirrels will know it and all the elephants will know it." [3] The squirrels may have *legal* sovereignty, but only the elephants have *political* sovereignty. Legal sovereignty is the right of a nation to pursue its policies without asking permission of another. Political sovereignty is the capacity to exercise this right. To assert that the United States and the Soviet Union have political sovereignty is not to say that either is omnipotent.

The drama of world politics is an intense, unending and universal struggle of power and purpose among men and nations. World politics, like all politics, is both personal and impersonal. It is personal because politicians and statesmen are persons and because their decisions always affect persons. Today millions of persons are profoundly affected by single political decisions, such as President Truman's intervention in Korea in 1950 or President Eisenhower's condemnation of British and French intervention in Egypt in 1956. World politics is impersonal because men and nations are often swept along by great historical forces over which they have little control, and because foreign policy decisions are made by the governments of nation-states which can hardly be described as personal.

International politics involves a constant struggle of power against power in a world of many nation-states which differ greatly in history, language, culture, political structure, purpose, size and might. Each state tries to maintain or to increase its power and status in relation to other states. Power is the capacity to achieve desired ends. Power in the political realm is similar to energy in the physical world or money in the economic world. Power as such is amoral. It can be used for good or evil. But men and nations which hold great power are always tempted to use it for narrow, selfish, and destructive ends. It is not infrequent that one man's power results in the domination or exploitation of another. The freedom conferred upon a man or a group of men may, by reason of the power they hold, mean loss of freedom for those from whom they draw their power or for others who interfere with its exercise. It is not only the Hitlers and Stalins who use other men as the instruments of their will. All men who hold political power, however nobly motivated they may be, are tempted to and sometimes do use other men for their own ends.

The power of a nation is its total capacity to achieve certain desired objectives. This capacity is determined by a variety of interrelated moral and material factors. The moral ingredients of national power include the fundamental values, beliefs, habits, and attitudes which make up the national character of a people. The concepts of justice and freedom which are cherished and practiced, the habits of democracy and fair play, and the attitudes toward the rights and welfare of peoples beyond our borders are elements of the American character which vitally affect our power and influence in the world. Slogans such as "unconditional surrender" and "manifest destiny," which express the mood of a people, play an important role. Deeds which affirm or deny what we say we believe affect our capacity to win friends and influence nations. Compare, for example, the effect upon the peoples of Asia and Africa of an American lynching with that of the Supreme Court's decision outlawing public school segregation.

Among the material factors which determine national power are the size and vocational diversity of the population, industrial potential, the general level of economic activity, the number of students pursuing technical or scientific education in college, the size and location of the nation's territories, and, of course, the state of military preparedness. These and other factors combine to determine not only the nation's war-making capacity but the nation's capacity to enlist and keep reliable allies.

World politics is vastly more than a struggle of power against power. If it were only that, there would be no point in discussing the relation between ethics and foreign policy. While might often makes "right," it is equally true that right, in terms of moral purpose and values, often affects the aims, character, and effect of might. Since international politics always involves the struggle of interest against interest, purpose against purpose, ethics is an inescapable factor in all foreign policy decisions. National power can be used to support policies which contribute to greater justice, peace and security; or it can be made the instrument of injustice, aggression and exploitation. The national purpose may be defined in terms which rule out the interests and rights of other nations, or in terms which take these interests into account. The significant moral difference between the governments of two nations has nothing to do with the quantity of power each possesses; it has everything to do with the quality of the purposes to which the power of each is committed, the appropriateness of the means employed to pursue this purpose, and the effect of these means on persons at home and abroad.

Many Americans, especially those who regard themselves as leaders of the Judaeo-Christian tradition, are reluctant to admit that power is a permanent and inescapable element in politics. They often use the phrase "power politics" as an instrument of condemnation for domestic or foreign policies they oppose. In the late 1930's many churchmen castigated President Roosevelt's efforts to strengthen America's military defenses as sheer "power politics." Several years ago when the United States refused to support a move in the United Nations Security Council to have the French-Tunisian dispute discussed, some church leaders accused their government of "power politics." When used as a term of reproach these words are at best imprecise; at worst they reveal a serious misunderstanding of the nature of international politics itself. Taken literally, the term "power politics" is an accurate but redundant statement of fact—all politics are power politics because in all politics power is an inescapable element.

Added to power and purpose, all politics includes a third element—*effect*, which is crucial from the viewpoint of moral judgment. All national political decisions have consequences for men and nations. These consequences may be good or evil, or, as in most situations, a complicated mixture of both. The actual effect of a particular policy may or may not be in harmony with the intentions which motivated that policy. The good intentions of statesmen are often sold short by their unwise and inappropriate policies. When Prime Minister Chamberlain negotiated with Hitler at Munich his intention was peace in our time, but the immediate effect of his unwise statesmanship was the encouragement of further German expansion and the long-term consequence may well have been World War II. Good intentions are not only sold short by unwise policies, but are often frustrated by the larger forces of history before which the most nobly-conceived and skillfully-executed policies are of little avail. From a moral standpoint, nevertheless, every foreign policy or series of policies must be judged both by its intentions and its consequences at home and abroad. To be morally responsible in the fullest sense a statesman must be motivated by legitimate foreign policy objectives, have the political wisdom to choose policies which will advance them, and the moral courage to pursue these policies even in the face of opposition.

When we use terms like legitimate, right, and good, we imply a standard of judgment, a point of reference beyond the realm of international politics. For adherents of Christianity and Judaism that point of reference is God and God's will for men as it is understood by the Judaeo-Christian tradition. Few Americans would dispute the moral desirability of the social goals of justice, freedom, peace, and respect for persons which are rooted in the religious heritage of Western civilization. The acceptance of these ideal ends is not the sum, but only the beginning of moral wisdom and responsibility. Our objectives in national and international life, like human aspirations generally, tend to be unlimited, but the means available for reaching these goals are severely rationed. If politics is the "art of the possible," as Bismarck said, political ethics is the art of achieving morally justified objectives within this realm of the possible. It is in the highly limited arena of available alternatives that the hard problems of both politics and ethics must be wrestled with. Ethics is a discipline of means, not of ends.

What is Foreign Policy?

Foreign policy is the sum total of a nation's efforts to affect the world beyond the borders of its legal jurisdiction. A foreign policy stratagem is always undertaken in order to influence the behavior or attitudes of the government or the people of other nations. All the efforts of our government to contain the Soviet Union, to strengthen Great Britain, to stabilize France, or to keep Egypt from going Communist fall within the realm of foreign policy. All nations seek constantly to realize their interests by influencing other nations through the various instruments of foreign policy—diplomatic, psychological, economic, and military.

The means available to any nation for influencing the policies of other nations are highly limited, although a more powerful nation has more means at its disposal than one less powerful. In domestic affairs within a well-ordered state the intention of a particular governmental policy usually bears some positive relation to the actual consequences of that policy. In international politics the intention of a national policy is often highly qualified or entirely frustrated by powerful external forces over which the nation has little or no control. The effectiveness of American foreign policy, and all foreign policy, is limited *externally* by the power, purpose and unpredictability of hostile nations, allies and uncommitted peoples; the weight of tradition and precedent; the inexorable facts of international economic life; and the vicissitudes of history generally.

Among the *internal* factors which further limit the foreign policy alternatives open to our government are the policy predisposition and resiliency of the party in power; the character, integrity, and political philosophy of the President and Secretary of State; the unending stream of information and advice which flows from experts in the State Department, the Department of Defense, Central Intelligence Agency, and other sources in and outside of government; the action or inaction of the Congress; the influence of pressure groups; the views of the press; and the demands and expectations of the public generally.[4]

The foreign policy objectives demanded by the public tend to be unlimited, but the means available to the policy makers are always severely restricted. Further, the citizens often insist upon contradictory goals like peace *and* security when the historical situation presents only the alternatives of a peace of tyranny or security through war. This was the case in 1940 and 1941 when most Americans wanted President Roosevelt to keep the United States out of war. These same Americans wanted other things such as prosperity and national security. But the world between Munich and Pearl Harbor did not offer the luxury of both peace and security. American security could be maintained only by risking and eventually engaging in war. The contradictory demands of the public, which made life so difficult for our policy makers, were decisively resolved by the surprise Japanese attack on December 7, 1941.

The Role of the "National Interest"

One of the central responsibilities of the government of any nation is to defend the nation against both internal and external enemies. National defense involves not only the preservation of the nation as a territorial and political entity, but the maintenance of the values the nation represents and the quality of collective and individual life possible within it. Each nation can be said to have a national purpose, a reason for its existence, which is based upon the central values held by the majority of its people. The government is morally bound to honor these basic values. The purpose of one nation may be to develop a national community based on justice and mutual respect and to pursue a foreign policy that makes for justice and security in the world of nations. The purpose of another nation may be to develop a tightly-organized state geared for the conquest of other states.

Each government defines the *national interest* in terms of the national purpose and in the light of the facts of world politics. The national interest is a calculation which attempts to relate moral values and political necessity. The government's understanding of the national interest embraces a series of objectives or commitments which are designed to contribute to the nation's central purpose. America's national purpose, it can be said, is to preserve and improve a society based upon consent and mutual respect and to help to create an international climate in which government by consent can take root and flourish. Flowing from this central purpose are more specific national interests such as the maintenance of a strong free-world coalition designed to frustrate Soviet aggression or subversion. Our grand strategy and finally our tactics are drawn from our understanding of our national interests. Every element of a sound United States foreign policy, whether it be an inconsequential procedural vote in the United Nations General Assembly or the initiation of the Truman Doctrine, is, by definition, related to our grand strategy, to our national interest, and finally to our national purpose. Both domestic and foreign policies should be enlisted in the service of the national purpose and the values that purpose represents.

Many Americans regard it as immoral to use the national interest as a guide to foreign policy. President Woodrow Wilson said: "It is a very perilous thing to determine the foreign policy of a nation in terms of the material interest. It is not only unfair to those with whom you are dealing, but it is degrading as regards your own actions." The difficulty with Wilson's statement is that the "material interest," which includes such mundane objectives as the maintenance of territorial integrity, is inextricably bound up with such trans-material objectives as the preservation of religious liberty and freedom of assembly.

The pursuit of national interests is wrong only when these interests are not true to the central national purpose or when the national purpose is itself morally unjustifiable. It is one thing for Germans to support national interests and objectives as defined by the Nazi government. It is quite another thing for Germans to support the national objectives as understood by the Bonn Government of 1957. If the national purpose of the United States is conceived in terms broad enough to take into account the interests and rights of other peoples and nations, and if our more specific interests are appropriate to this purpose, it is morally right for our government to pursue a foreign policy based upon the national interest.

The national interest can never be allowed to become the sole guide for foreign policy because governments and their peoples are always tempted to define that interest in narrow and ultimately self-defeating terms. Morally concerned citizens must constantly strive to develop an understanding of the national interest which takes into account legitimate national values such as security and supra-national values such as international peace. It should be borne in mind, however, that the President of the United States is directly responsible only for the security of our nation and for the preservation of the values we, as a people, represent. He is not responsible in the same direct way for the security of Britain, France or India, although if he is morally sensitive and politically wise he will recognize that in our interdependent world the security of these countries is not unrelated to the security of the United States and, for that matter, to international peace itself.

The President is charged with the responsibility of defending the national interest against narrow sub-national interests when there is a conflict between the two. He must, of course, take sub-national interests into account in order to gain consent for policies he ultimately adopts and because, in a democracy, the diversity represented by interest groups is cherished rather than suppressed.

Statesmanship is the art of reconciling or accommodating the competing claims of national, supra-national and sub-national interests and values. Setting tariff rates is a simple example of what is always a complex political and moral task. The Wisconsin dairy industry (a sub-national interest) wants higher tariffs imposed against Danish cheese. The health of the over-all United States economy (a national interest), and of the free-world economy (both an American national interest and a supra-national interest) is usually hurt by higher tariffs. It would appear that a statesman dedicated to the national interest would have to oppose higher tariffs against imported cheese, even if the dairy industry in the United States would "suffer."

One could make a case for the proposition that in foreign policy genuine national interests should always have a higher moral claim than sub-national interests, although one would have to make a distinction between those sub-national interests which contribute to the national purpose and those which tend to violate or compromise the national purpose. What is good for Standard Oil or the AFL-CIO may or may not be good for the country. It depends upon the effect of the particular interest on the general interest.

The moral admonition that supra-national claims should always enjoy a priority over national interests is of little help to the statesman who is charged, not with the responsibility of maintaining world peace, but with the task of defending his nation. Perhaps the best advice citizens can give to their political leaders is to urge them to pursue policies the leaders believe will best serve the national interest. These same citizens should do everything possible to broaden the nation's understanding of and commitment to foreign policies which show a decent respect for the opinions and rights of mankind. The restraint and criticism of other nations, including friend and foe, can sometimes prevent a government from pursuing politically unwise and morally indefensible policies.

On the deepest level there may be a concurrence between legitimate national and supra-national interests and values, but on the level of everyday politics the interests of the various nations are in constant conflict. Perhaps legitimate sub-national interests can also be harmonized with legitimate national interests. This is not to say that what is good for General Motors is good for the United States or what is good for the United States is good for the world. We are merely suggesting that on the deepest level *legitimate* interests in these three areas can probably be brought into some degree of harmony or accommodation.

The clash of national interests is a central and permanent characteristic of the contemporary nation-state system. Governments persist in pursuing objectives which are incompatible with the goals of other governments. The sharpest and most dangerous conflicts arise when nations pursue policies contrary to widely accepted standards of international morality as defined, for example, by the Charter of the United Nations. The Communist attack in South Korea in 1950 was such a violation. But even when nations pursue "legitimate" and morally defensible goals, international conflict is inevitable. From our point of view the goals of freedom from colonialism and protection against tyranny are equally desirable, and yet we see in the Middle East how policies calculated to support these laudable goals are in constant conflict.

Political conflict, domestic or international, is rooted in the nature of man. It is a reflection of his finitude, his moral weakness, and his irrationality. If the presuppositions of the Biblical understanding of human nature are correct, there will always be conflicts of power and interest among men and nations. This struggle of power and pride cannot be exorcised by pleas for goodwill, by education, by social engineering, or by technology. With moral insight, humility, and political wisdom, conflict can be mitigated, beguiled, and often made to serve a higher common interest than the immediate narrow, particular interests involved. It is the solemn duty of responsible statesmen and morally concerned citizens to seek the points at which conflicting interests can be compromised without serious loss to the most vital of the legitimate claims. The best we can expect is a rough justice, an unstable equilibrium, and an uneasy truce.

Biblical Religion and Politics

One's understanding of international politics and foreign policy is not only drawn from the study of history, political science, and current affairs, but is a reflection of what one basically believes about the nature of man and history. These beliefs in turn influence one's interpretation of what one learns from study and observation. The foregoing interpretation of international politics is instructed by certain basic assumptions of the Judaeo-Christian religion which will be noted briefly below.

Biblical religion is expressed both in the imperative and declarative mood. Its imperative "thou shalt" is always accompanied by the declaration of who God is, what man is, and what God has done for man. The Bible declares what *is* and what *ought to be*. It asks and answers two questions of central concern to our understanding of ethics and politics—"What is the human situation?" and "What is the duty of man?" An understanding of what *is* is a prerequisite for understanding what *ought to be*. An understanding of who God is and what God has done for man is the basis for understanding what God requires of man.

The morally-concerned reformer and the political idealist often become, in their zeal, so preoccupied with the imperatives of human responsibility that they ignore the givenness of human existence. Ignorance of the limits and possibilities of man and history has often led to utopian crusades which have ended in disaster. The long road from Versailles to Pearl Harbor and beyond is cluttered with the whitened bones of crusades that failed—the League of Nations, peace through economic planning, the Kellogg-Briand Pact, and peace through the renunciation of war, to name but a few. These crusades, in which American religious leaders invested so much energy and devotion, failed not for lack of good intentions or enthusiasm but because the crusaders tended to believe that morally desirable goals were, for the mere fact of their desirability, politically possible. They misread current history because they failed to understand the tragedies and contingencies of the whole realm of history. They misunderstood history because they did not understand the limits and possibilities of human nature.

Biblical religion, as understood by the preponderance of its interpreters, embraces certain basic affirmations about the nature and destiny of man which contribute to our understanding of the human situation in general and of politics in particular. These affirmations, summarized briefly here, are but a part of a much larger complex of belief and cannot be fully understood apart from it.

First, Biblical religion asserts that God is the Lord of history, the creator, sustainer and redeemer of mankind, the judge of men and of nations. God, not man, is the measure of all things. The ultimate destiny of man and nations, it is affirmed, is in the hands of a God of life and love, whose purposes and ways can never be fully comprehended.

Second, God wills that all men should love Him with their whole hearts and treat other men as brothers. In social terms this means that men should live together in a community in which each person, unprevented by the contravening acts of government, may develop the gifts of mind, body, and spirit with which God has endowed him. Such a community, whether local, national, or international, is characterized by justice, freedom and mutual helpfulness.

Third, the Bible asserts that man, the most exalted and complex of God's creations, is capable of good and evil. This moral capacity is made possible by both man's limited freedom and his ability to reason. He is free, within the limits set by nature and history, to respond in obedience or disobedience to the will of his Creator. Though he is always tempted to respond in disobedience, such disobedience is not imposed from without by a cruel destiny or by society, but springs from within—from human pride, inordinate self-regard and the inclination to pursue self-interest at the expense of the interests and rights of other men. Human reason supplies the capacity to comprehend the interests and welfare of one's neighbor, but reason does not provide the will or the capacity to love him. Reason is not an independent agency which transcends the self, but is rather a servant of the self. It can be enlisted in man's rebellion against God as well as in his obedience to Him. All men fall short of God's will for them, but God's grace and forgiveness are yet available. At times some men are able, by the grace of God, to overcome narrow self-interest and to act on behalf of a larger and nobler self or of a community of selves. Man's nature, capable of good or evil, is morally ambiguous. As Reinhold Niebuhr has said, "Man's capacity for justice makes democracy possible; but man's inclination to injustice makes democracy necessary." [5] Man is not capable of perfect, disinterested love of his neighbor. But with the help of God and the moral restraints of the community, especially those imposed by a responsible government, man is capable of a measure of justice. Our faith that a measure of justice and order is possible within the realm of political necessity gives us hope without illusion and humility without despair.

Fourth, human history does not reveal its meaning; nor does it contain the means of its own fulfillment. According to Biblical faith history is neither "a tale told by an idiot" nor the arena of inevitable progress. History receives its meaning from God, the Lord of time and eternity. It begins and ends in God and its ultimate fulfillment awaits the end of history. On the vast stage of history men, "a little lower than the angels" and yet limited by "original sin," respond to God's will in obedience or disobedience. Since men are morally ambiguous history itself is morally ambiguous. Men are inclined to seek their own interests at the expense of the rights of others; hence there will always be a struggle of pride and power within and among nations. The problems of international conflict, war, insecurity, and tyranny are not thrust upon men from without. They are not the product of simple ignorance, ill will, social maladjustment, or any other external blemish. The international power struggle, observes George F. Kennan, flows "from certain facts about human nature—certain imperfections if you will—that are basic and are not going to be corrected by any man-made devices, whether institutional or educational." [6]

Conflicting interests are rooted in man's nature—his pride, his self-assertion, and his will persist until the end of time. The struggle of power and interest is unceasing. Sometimes the forces of relative justice push ahead in one sector of the battlefield, only to be forced into retreat by the legions of injustice. There are episodes of grandeur and nobility. There are deeds of cruelty and brutality. The battle within history is never wholly won and never wholly lost. New and fresh opportunities for justice and nobility have a way of appearing when a battle seems almost lost. There is no final victory or redemption within history, but according to the Judaeo-Christian faith God's high purposes will ultimately be fulfilled.

No citizen, statesman, political party or government is ever the embodiment of perfect justice or righteousness. And none is ever wholly evil. History is not like a Western movie in which the "bad guys" are easily distinguished from the "good guys," because the "bad guys" wear dark hats. In any political struggle there is some justice and some injustice on each side. A recognition of this universal involvement in self-interest and pride leads some people to a moral cynicism which prevents them from perceiving that relative justice is the very heart of both ethics and politics. President Truman's decision to intervene in Korea was not based upon the assumption that the United States and South Korea represented perfect justice and that North Korea was the personification of injustice. It was based rather on a discriminating judgment about the relative justice of each side as well as on prudential considerations, such as the security of the United States and the free world. Neither of these considerations ruled out Mr. Truman's genuine interest in international peace and security. Hans J. Morgenthau has summed up the problem in these words: "To act successfully . . . is political wisdom. To know with despair that the political act is inevitably evil, and to act nevertheless, is moral courage. To choose among several expedient actions the least evil one is moral judgment. In the combination of political wisdom, moral courage, and moral judgment, man reconciles his political nature with his moral destiny." [7]

*Two Approaches to Ethics and Foreign
Policy*

Since the turn of the present century the dominant
approach to international politics in America has
emphasized the rationality and moral capacity of man
and the possibility of continuous or cumulative progress in history. This approach, which has instructed a
great number of religious leaders, has emphasized the
ideal goals of international peace, justice, and broth-
erhood. Advocates of this approach often insisted
upon an absolute ethic based exclusively upon goodwill, noncoercion, cooperation, and education. This
approach, both in its liberal humanist and religious
versions, is rooted in the rationalism of the eighteenth
and nineteenth centuries which believed in human
perfectability and historic progress.

Since the mid-thirties this dominant "liberal" approach has been challenged by an increasing number
of theologians, students of world politics, and statesmen who, although no less concerned about international peace and justice, have emphasized the limits
of man's moral capacity and the tragic character of
history. Among the critics of liberal idealism the
names of Reinhold Niebuhr, Hans J. Morgenthau,
and George F. Kennan are perhaps best known. These
men and others who share their general approach to
international politics are sometimes referred to as
"realists." They criticize the dominant approach because it is "utopian," overly "optimistic," and "legalistic." The "idealists" sometimes charge the "realists"
with cynicism and failure of nerve. (There are, of
course, many persons who do not fit neatly into either
camp because they embrace elements of both.)

More important than the labels which are used to

characterize these two basic approaches to foreign policy are their fundamental similarities and differences. Morally concerned and religiously committed persons in both groups believe in the sovereignty of God over all men and nations and in the moral necessity of pursuing goals which transcend any narrow conception of the national interest. Both groups accept the "law of love" as the ultimate standard of moral behavior, although they apply it differently to the decisions of politics.

Perhaps the basic difference between the two lies in their understanding of what is politically possible, especially in the foreseeable future. Those with a more optimistic view of man and history tend to insist upon political objectives in domestic and international life which have no approximate historical precedents, which enjoy little continuity with the present political situation, and which rely heavily upon man's rationality and capacity for altruism. They tend to regard ideal goals, such as universal disarmament and a democratic world government, as political possibilities in the foreseeable future. The "realists" who emphasize man's morally ambiguous nature and the tragic elements in history are content with more limited political objectives. The "realists" may have the same ultimate goals as the "liberal idealists," but the former tend to regard these ultimate goals as "ideal ends" which lend perspective and hope, while the latter tend to regard them both as "ideal ends" and achievable political objectives. Instead of a pure ethic of absolute ends, the "realist" talks about an "ethic of responsibility" which calls for a choice among available political alternatives, none of which is wholly pure or just. To the charge that this is an "ethic of compromise," the "realist" acknowledges that it is, but insists that choosing the lesser of two evils or the greater of two goods is more responsible than an ethic of abstention which, in the name of purity, often leads to political behavior indistinguishable from that of the moral cynic.

The "utopians" tend to give priority attention to symbols of the international community we would all like to see realized. They emphasize "international law," universal codes and international machinery designed to qualify or eliminate national sovereignty. The "idealist" tends to be more concerned with activities at the United Nations than with the policies of the State Department.

The "realists," on the other hand, tend to give priority to more limited foreign policy objectives such as a broader definition of the national interest, regional defense alliances in the face of the Soviet threat, and military and economic aid to our allies in the non-Soviet world. These more limited objectives call upon man's egoistic, as well as his altruistic capacities, and enjoy a direct continuity with the present historical situation. [8]

The discussion thus far and that which follows is written from the perspective of a morally-concerned "realist" who believes realism to afford a more authentic reading of the central Judaeo-Christian tradition than the perspective of the "utopians." American liberal idealism, including its Christian and Jewish manifestations, seems to be more closely related to eighteenth- and nineteenth-century secular thought than to the views of the ancient Hebrew prophets, the early Christian church, the Medieval church, or the teachings of the Reformers. The present writer also believes that "realist" assumptions about the nature of man and history are confirmed by the experience of statesmen, the findings of social scientists and psychologists, and the everyday political events we encounter in the pages of our newspapers. Further, he believes this perspective offers not only a greater understanding of what is, but a surer guide to what ought to be.

The Limits of Faith and Theology in Politics

At the beginning of this chapter we noted that the official justification for the supreme irony of November 2, 1956, was morality. Our government joined, in the name of high moral principles, our arch enemies in helping to destroy the influence of our friends in the Middle East. Is this not an eloquent example of the fact that morality and faith can be sources of confusion as well as of wisdom in politics? Man's moral sense can be the cause of immorality and self-deception just as man's religious views can be the source of confusion and self-righteousness. The root of perplexity is the ambiguity of man. Man seeks moral justification precisely because he has a moral sense. But man's interests, acknowledged or unacknowledged, often tempt man to clothe his vices in the garments of virtue, to pursue narrow interests in the name of humanity, to make moral principles the servants of self-interest. As John Adams expressed it: "Our passions, ambitions, avarice, love and resentment . . . possess so much metaphysical subtlety and so much overpowering eloquence that they insinuate themselves into the understanding and the conscience and convert both to their party."

How can religion be made a source of wisdom rather than of confusion? There is no easy answer. It is too simple, although partially true, to say that wrong religion or false theology leads to confusion and that the right theology leads to understanding.

Most Americans approach politics pragmatically, rather than theoretically. Explicit political doctrine or theory is not a part of the working equipment of the majority of our political leaders. Yet all of us do have certain acknowledged or unacknowledged assumptions about the nature of man, history, and politics which do in fact influence our understanding of international politics and foreign policy. This book is based on the premise that it is useful to examine critically one's implicit assumptions to see if they help or hinder one's effort to relate ethics to foreign policy. It is quite possible, of course, for a statesman or an ordinary citizen to have a profound and morally sensitive understanding of foreign policy without subscribing to any explicit theological creed. Other things being equal, however, this writer believes that a recognition of the central affirmations of the Judaeo-Christian faith will deepen one's awareness of the complexities and ambiguities, as well as the opportunities, of international politics and will help deliver one from utopian illusions on the one hand and cynical despair on the other.

CHAPTER TWO

America alone and isolated cannot assure even its own security. We must be joined by the capability and resolution of nations that have proved themselves dependable defenders of freedom. Isolation from them invites war.

DWIGHT D. EISENHOWER, JANUARY 10, 1957

PEACE, SECURITY AND THE COLD WAR

On Sunday morning, December 7, 1941, Japan launched a surprise attack on our Pearl Harbor naval base in Hawaii. In one hour and fifty minutes nineteen ships were sunk or disabled, one hundred and twenty American planes were destroyed, 2,335 soldiers and sailors and 68 civilians were killed. On December 8 the United States Congress, with one dissenting vote, declared war on Japan. Three days later, after Germany and Italy had declared war on the United States, our government recognized a state of war to exist with them as well. Within a matter of days we were full-fledged participants in a great war which was to end four years and several millions of casualties later with the dropping of two atomic bombs on Japan.

In early 1941 most Americans wanted both peace *and* national security, but the unyielding world of 1941 offered fulfillment of one or the other objective, not both. We had to choose between a peace of capitulation or a war to defend our national security. Before

27

we had fully made up our minds, the Pearl Harbor attack resolved the dilemma of our mutually exclusive demands. We went to war because we were attacked and because our security and independence as a nation were gravely imperiled. Although our security had been threatened long before Pearl Harbor, the attack dramatized the fact which most Americans were reluctant to accept. The United States responded to Pearl Harbor as any nation in a similar situation would respond. No nation wishes to be conquered, subdued, or enslaved by another power. All nations want to maintain their territorial integrity, their security, and the values represented by that security. When their security and survival are threatened nations fight back with all the weapons at their disposal, subject only to the restraints of prudence and, on occasion, moral scruple. When a nation is confronted with a choice between the imposition of tyranny and war, it will choose war even when it has but the slightest chance of resisting the aggressor successfully. Sometimes it will fight when it has no chance of success at all; witness the Netherlands, which fought back bitterly when attacked by Nazi Germany in 1940, although the possibility of success was almost nil. In this case not security, but the mingled ends of self-preservation and self-respect prevailed.

What Is National Security?

The government of any nation has the moral responsibility to defend the security of the nation and the values for which the nation stands. A nation is secure when its people can pursue their daily life with a reasonable expectation that the values they cherish most highly will be defended against enemies both internal and external. A secure people do not live in constant fear that their government may be subverted, their nation invaded, their homes bombed, or their men killed in battle.

Security and peace are not the same thing. A people can be at peace and at the same time be desperately afraid of what the morrow might bring. Czechoslovakia and Hungary are presently at peace, but the people of these countries are by no means secure. The United States is at peace, but we are not fully secure. Although we have more direct control over our national destiny than the peoples in Soviet satellites, our national security is threatened by the existence of a powerful and militant Soviet Union.

Absolute security is not a possibility in this world. Insecurity has always been the lot of men and nations, but it is probably true to say that today mankind lives under the shadow of greater insecurity than ever before. As Thomas E. Murray, a member of the United States Atomic Energy Commission, observed: "Presently we are no longer secure about the one thing that always in the past was secure. Amid wars, pestilences and famines, mankind has always been assured of one thing—that there would be a mankind living here on earth until the day on which man's temporal history would be terminated by an act of Almighty God. We no longer have this elementary security. Man now has the power to put an end to his own history. In its effort to protect the freedom of the world, America has invented nuclear weapons capable of destroying all human life." [1]

The great majority of Americans believe their country to be worth defending and worth defending by military means. The tiny minority who believe that military action is never justified nevertheless agree with other morally-concerned citizens that we have a national responsibility for making our country worthy of preservation. This minority also agrees that the nation should be defended, but by other than military means. There have been instances in recent history when citizens did not regard their government as morally worthy of defense. During World War II some Germans worked and prayed for the defeat of their government because they believed that Nazism had made it unworthy of defense. During the Korean War thousands of North Korean and Chinese soldiers surrendered to United Nations forces and refused to be repatriated at the war's end because they were convinced that the chances for a full and free life were better under the government of the "enemy" than under their own. Moreover, people under severe provocation may feel so strongly opposed to their own government as to attempt to overthrow it by armed revolt. The October 1956 revolt in Hungary is the most recent example of citizens who were willing to give their lives in order to overthrow a tyrannical and corrupt regime. Unhappily, their efforts did not succeed.

The Cold War

In April 1947 Bernard Baruch said, "Let us not be deceived—we are today in the midst of a cold war." His solemn words are still true. The term "cold war" is a popular but fairly accurate way to characterize the postwar bipolar struggle between the Communist world, under the leadership of the Soviet Union, and the "free world," under the leadership of the United States. A cold war, no less than a hot one, is a threat to national security and international peace. The bipolar struggle is, moreover, aggravated by a vast revolutionary upheaval in Asia and Africa. The East-West power struggle and the ferment in the areas recently or still under Western control are separate and yet interrelated political realities. Each would exist without the other, but each has greatly affected the character of the other. The role of India, for example, in the Cold War, is accentuated precisely because she does not want to take sides in the Cold War. The recent visits of Prime Minister Nehru to Moscow and to Washington dramatize the fact that both the Soviet Union and the United States are attempting to solicit the tacit, if not the explicit, support of India.

The Cold War is not simply a struggle between two rival power blocs. It is that indeed, but it is more. It is a struggle between two different ways of organizing society. The United States and most of her free-world allies believe in, and to a considerable extent practice, the principle of government by the willing and active consent of the governed. The Soviet Union is ruled by a small clique which wrests an unwilling consent from the governed by employing instruments of fear and coercion. In the first decade after World War II the Soviets have imposed this same rigid form of political control directly on their European satellites and indirectly, by influence and example, upon China. As of 1957 only one Soviet satellite, Yugoslavia, had succeeded in freeing itself from Moscow's grip, although the October 1956 revolution in Poland has apparently gained for that country a measure of genuine independence. The immediate future of Poland remains, however, uncertain.

The moral and political differences between the Communist and the non-Communist worlds are significant, but they cannot be characterized accurately in absolute terms. There are serious moral contradictions within the free world and elements of justice within the Soviet-Chinese world. The term "free world" does not mean that all nations in the Western coalition have free and democratic governments, although many of them do. It means rather that these nations are free from external domination. Even within the most democratic of them there are elements of unfreedom and injustice. In the United States treatment of the Negro, although it has changed substantially in recent years, must be greatly improved before all Negro citizens enjoy full equality of opportunity. Due to poverty and other factors millions of Americans still do not receive a sound education, adequate medical care, or full protection under the law. We have, as a nation, a great deal of unfinished business. If we remain true to our highest values there will always be unfinished business, although the priorities on the agenda will change from time to time.

In spite of our obvious shortcomings, we should not indulge in easy equations between our sins and the sins of the Communist world, unless the sins in question are in fact comparable. Our racial discrimination, which is contrary to the highest law of the land and to our own professed values, should not be morally equated with the officially-sponsored slave labor system of the Soviet Union. Nor should incidents of police brutality in the United States be morally equated with the extensive policy of "brainwashing" in Red China. Taking all internal contradictions into account, there remains a profound moral difference between the quality of individual and collective life possible under Soviet-Chinese Communism on the one hand and Western democracy on the other. This difference is eloquently demonstrated by the flow of refugees and escapees through the Iron and Bamboo Curtains during the past ten years. In 1955 alone 271,000 persons fled from East Germany to the West. Only a small percentage of this number have "fled" in the other direction. In 1956 and 1957 tens of thousands of men, women and children fled from re-Stalinized Hungary to the West. The welcome-home campaigns of the Soviet Union and her satellites have not made a substantial change in this refugee picture.

The moral difference between the Soviet and the free world is also evident in the foreign policies of each. Since the end of World War II the Soviet regime has pursued a vigorous policy of political and territorial expansion by subversion, military threat and, in the case of Korea, outright military agression. With the conquest of China, imperial Communism has swallowed up ten once independent nations, doubling its territory and the number of subjects under its rule. The new Sino-Russian empire covers almost the entire Eurasian land mass, stretching from Berlin to the Straits of Formosa. When the Soviet bloc consummated its arms deal with Egypt in 1955, Moscow had brought to the threshold of realization the old Czarist ambition of becoming a major power in the Mediterranean world.

The West, in marked contrast to the Soviet Union, has been rapidly divesting itself of its colonial territories in Asia and Africa. Since 1945 nineteen new independent states have been born and no fewer than 600,000,000 people have been freed from Western rule. The colonial policies of France and Belgium may not have been as wise or as morally sensitive as those of Britain and the United States, but with the growing nationalism in Africa and the Middle East no power can continue to pursue old-style colonial policies with impunity. The question is not whether the imperial powers should withdraw, but when and how. Not all departures will be as graceful as the transfer of power from Britain to India in 1947 or from Britain to Ghana a decade later.

But colonialism is not dead. Only the old-fashioned Western colonialism has disappeared. The new Soviet imperialism is very much alive and on the march. Made bold by its successful conquests in the first decade after World War II, imperial Communism relentlessly pursues its objectives of political and ideological expansion in Europe, Asia, and the Middle East. The United States, by virtue of her technology and the power bequeathed to her by World War II, is the leader of the free-world coalition which is united by its determination to prevent further Communist expansion. The Cold War between these two morally and politically conflicting forces is unremitting and its battles are fought in the Security Council of the United Nations, in the divided city of Berlin, in the rice paddies of Indo-China, on the shores of the Mediterranean, and in the minds of men everywhere.

The Denunciation and Rehabilitation of Stalin

After the death of Stalin in 1953, many people in the West looked for a thaw in the Cold War. There was some evidence of relaxation of tensions, but the change was not dramatic. Then came the startling denunciation of Stalin by Soviet Party Chief Krushchev at the Communist Party Congress in Moscow in February of 1956. Some Americans were quick to believe that this presaged the end of the Cold War. There were some hopeful developments in the satellites. Poland succeeded in achieving greater national independence. Any illusory hopes that the men of the Kremlin had foresworn the ways of Stalin were brought to an abrupt end, however, in the blood bath of Budapest in October 1956, less than a year after Stalinism had been renounced. There is no convincing evidence to indicate that the present ruling elite in Moscow has given up either the Stalinist goal of world domination or Stalinist tactics for reaching that goal. On November 18, 1956, after Hungary was again safely under the Kremlin's heel, Krushchev said to Western diplomats at a Moscow reception: "Whether you like it or not, history is on our side! We will bury you yet!" At the Kremlin's New Year's Eve party six weeks later he said, "We are all Stalinists" when it comes to fighting imperialism. He praised Stalin as "a great fighter against imperialism" and "a great Marxist." These statements were accompanied by a tightening of control over the Eastern European satellites. The speedy rehabilitation of Stalin came as no surprise to those aware that in his original speech attacking the brutality and megalomania of Stalin, Krushchev reaffirmed the Communist goal of world conquest and criticized Stalinist tactics only when they were directed against Party comrades.

To say that Stalin has been rehabilitated is not to say that there is not a new flexibility in Soviet strategy and tactics. There is considerable evidence to indicate that its ultimate goal of world conquest may be pursued now and in the immediate future by means somewhat different from those on which Stalin placed primary reliance. There is no evidence to suggest that the Soviet Union has abandoned her traditional methods of ideological penetration or internal subversion or her reliance on nuclear weapons, guided missiles, submarines or long-range bombers. It would appear rather that in addition to her regular arsenal of military and political weapons, she will make an increasing use of economic and psychological weapons. Her new efforts to stimulate trade, economic aid and technical assistance, and the highly-publicized junkets of Krushchev and Bulganin to strategic capitals are not a substitute for, but rather a supplement to, the more belligerent methods of the recent past. In the process of the Soviet downgrading and rehabilitating of Stalin and Stalinism, it would appear that the danger to the free world has actually increased.

The Cold War continues, although its character has been somewhat changed by political developments within the Soviet Union. Its character probably has been affected even more by the so-called "nuclear stalemate" between the Soviet world and the free world. The recognition on both sides that a nuclear holocaust could mean the end of civilization as we know it may contribute to what Sir Winston Churchill has called a "peace of mutual terror." In any event, we have been and will continue for some time to be in an era of "competitive coexistence" and we hope that the chances of this competition remaining peaceful have been considerably enhanced by the threat of possible mutual annihilation. It should be noted that there is nothing automatic about the mutual deterrent effect of a growing nuclear arsenal on each side. The "nuclear stalemate" could quickly cease to exist if one side attained decisive superiority in nuclear weapons, means of delivery, or even in conventional military strength. The "stalemate" depends upon a balance of power between the two blocs, regardless of the level at which the balance is maintained.

United States Security Objectives

To defend the territorial integrity of the United States, and the larger values we as a nation believe in, our government has defined three major security objectives: 1) to prevent the free world from being nibbled to death by piecemeal Communist expansion; 2) to prevent both "brushfire" wars and general nuclear war; 3) and, failing the second objective, to maintain a sufficiently powerful and diversified military program to win either "brushfire" or nuclear wars. The government seeks to achieve these foreign policy objectives primarily by making further Communist expansion both unattractive and unrewarding. From any rational or moral point of view it is far more desirable to deter future Soviet military action than it is to deal with it after it has already taken place. This primary strategy of deterrence is both a military and diplomatic task. Perhaps the Korean War could have been avoided if the West had maintained stronger military defenses in South Korea and had let it be known that we regarded our position there to be vital. While every appropriate military, diplomatic, economic, and psychological means should be enlisted in the policy of deterring aggression, we must also have the capacity to deal with aggression on a small or a large scale if our policy should fail. If there should be war, we want to be in a position to win.

Some writers have asserted that neither side would *win* in the event of a thermonuclear war. They admit that in spite of the unprecedented cost and massive mutual destruction of World War II, there were significant differences between the victor and the vanquished. A nuclear holocaust, they contend, would make a mockery of the word *victory*. In all probability both sides would suffer greatly in such a war. The victor might indeed emerge considerably worse off after his victory than before. But it is also true that the victor will be in a position to dominate the vanquished. This fact has both political and moral significance. Would there not be an important difference between the "peace terms" dictated by the Western alliance and those of the Soviet bloc? Would not the moral and political differences which now exist between the two camps persist, at least in part, into the postwar period, and would not these differences influence the character of the policies pursued by the victor, even if these policies were directed from and toward mere fragments of the civilization we now know?

National Security—Alone or with Others

Since the turn of the present century many Americans have dreamed of an ideal world in which the community of nations would be organized to keep the peace by collectively punishing any state which broke the peace or attempted to impose its will by force on another state or people. The League of Nations and the United Nations in turn have been regarded by some as the actual or potential instrument for accomplishing this purpose. According to this ideal arrangement the unilateral pursuit of national objectives by military means would be "illegal," and an attack against any nation would be regarded as an attack against all. Charles Burton Marshall has characterized this ideal of "collective security" as a "generalized notion of all nations banding together in undertaking a vague obligation to perform unspecified actions in response to hypothetical events brought on by some unidentifiable state." We need not pause here to discuss the achievability or the desirability of such an ideal arrangement. The important fact is that we do not now have and cannot in the foreseeable future anticipate the establishment of an effective universal agency for keeping the peace. [2]

Today and for many years to come the focus of political power and moral responsiblity in war and peace will rest where it has rested for the past three or more centuries—with the governments of nation-states. Each nation must decide how it will pursue its security policies. The United States has the theoretical choice of pursuing its foreign policy objectives in isolation from other nations or in cooperation with them. She cannot transfer the responsibility for her own security or for international security to a supra-national authority because no such authority exists.

There are some Americans who would like to escape the heavy foreign-policy responsibilities which have fallen upon our country. These people are not the geographical isolationists of the 1930's who pointed confidently to the "protection" of two vast oceans. They are the new moral isolationists who believe the price of international leadership to be too high or who regard the inescapable restraints of genuine international cooperation as an unjustifiable infringement on American sovereignty. Many of these present-day isolationists insist that the United States is powerful enough, wise enough and "good" enough to "go it alone." Senator John W. Bricker's proposed Constitutional amendment designed to curb the President's treaty-making power is a symbol of the new isolationism.

The majority of Americans believe that it is both necessary and desirable for our nation to defend its security in cooperation with other nations. Our homes, our lives and our national destinies are intertwined because we face a common external threat. The British political cartoonist, David Low, put it this way: "Ever since our British affairs got mixed up with yours and our lives and deaths became affected by what you do in America—and vice versa, let me point out—we fight your political issues as though they were our own, which, after all, they are. . . . Fate has made us all honorary Americans." [3] He is right— we rely on Britain and France as greatly as they do on us. America is not powerful enough, wise enough or virtuous enough to defend herself and to discharge her international responsibilities without the constant help and advice of her allies. Only those blinded by what Denis W. Brogan calls "the illusion of American omnipotence" or by what one may call "the illusion of American virtue" can fail to grasp this fact of political and moral interdependence.

Economically and technologically, the United States is dependent upon imports from abroad. If these imports were cut off or substantially reduced, our familiar daily life would be drastically changed and our defense program would collapse unless domestic substitutes could be found. [4]

Politically and militarily, our nation is dependent upon other nations. Our radar warning system and our Strategic Air Command, both widely dispersed throughout the world, would have to be pulled back into continental United States and a few American possessions if it were not for the cooperation of allies and other friendly countries in Europe, Asia and Latin America.

Morally, we need our allies and they need us. No nation has sufficient wisdom or virtue to go its own way without the counsel, criticism and moral restraint of other nations. The more powerful a nation is the more moral and political restraints are needed. A "minor" mistake or miscalculation of a superpower often has a tremendous impact on the security and welfare of other peoples. A small nation can afford to make a big mistake, but a big nation can not afford the luxury of even small mistakes. When a Secretary of State or a President, for example, makes statements about unleashing Chiang Kai-shek or liberating Soviet satellites, intended primarily for domestic consumption, he can unsettle trusted allies and even shake the Western coalition. Who knows to what extent the loose talk about liberating the satellites during our 1952 election campaign was responsible for the Budapest blood bath of 1956?

United States and the Free-World Coalition

When Secretary of State Hull returned from the Moscow Conference in 1943 at which Britain, the Soviet Union and the United States had agreed to create a postwar "international organization," he said there "will no longer be need for spheres of influence, for alliances, for balance of power, or any other of the special arrangements by which, in the unhappy past, the nations strove to safeguard their security or to promote their interests." Mr. Hull was not alone in his high hope. Many other Americans have looked upon the United Nations as an actual or potential substitute for the hard realities of world politics and the new international responsibilities of the United States.

The easy optimism in the United States about the United Nations was soon dashed by mounting evidence of Soviet expansion and intransigence in Europe. By early 1947 the United States government recognized that the United Nations was not capable of dealing with questions in which major interests of the Big Powers were at stake. President Truman initiated a series of specific commitments which, for the first time since the turn of the century, were based upon the realities of the world situation. The basic assumptions underlying these new commitments were that the United States has international responsibilities commensurate with her power and that her security could be defended only by helping to defend the security of other nations threatened by potential Soviet aggression. During the historic "fifteen weeks" between February 21, 1947, when the British informed us that they could no longer bolster up Greece and Turkey, and June 5, 1947, when the Secretary of State made a speech at Harvard University launching the Marshall Plan, American foreign policy underwent a revolutionary change.[5] During this brief period our government fully accepted the leadership of the free world which had been thrust upon us and took appropriate steps to build a viable Western coalition. It recognized the necessity of building adequate deterrent power to balance the power of the aggressive Soviet empire, especially in Europe. On March 12 President Truman launched a program of economic and military aid to defend Greece and Turkey against Soviet penetration and enunciated the Truman Doctrine of containing the Soviet Union. Then came the Marshall Plan, which was really the Lend-Lease program of the Cold War. The basic policy established during those "fifteen weeks" has been continued until the present time with no drastic modifications, unless one regards the Eisenhower Administration's "reliance on the United Nations" during the winter of 1956-1957 Suez crisis as a drastic departure from the policy of primary reliance on the Western coalition.

The most ambitious and far-reaching enterprise of the new American foreign policy was the establishment of the North Atlantic Treaty Organization. The agreement creating NATO was signed on April 4, 1949, by the United States, the United Kingdom, Canada, France, Italy, Belgium, the Netherlands, Luxembourg, Denmark, Norway, Iceland and Portugal. Subsequently, Greece, Turkey and the Federal Republic of Germany were added. A treaty with New Zealand and Australia followed in September 1951. The Southeast Asia Treaty was signed three years later by the United Kingdom, France, New Zealand, Australia, Thailand, Pakistan and the Philippines. We also have bilateral military treaties with the Philippines, Japan, the Republic of Korea, and the Republic of China (Formosa). Including the Rio Treaty of 1947, which embraces twenty-one American states, the United States as of 1957 was committed to the mutual military defense, under certain specified conditions, of forty-two foreign states. Some treaties, like NATO, commit us to immediate military action in the event of attack; others, like the Southeast Asia Treaty, commit us only to consultation.

Mutual Defense Alliances: Pro and Con

NATO and other defense alliances are sometimes criticized because their participants "bypass the United Nations" in matters covered by their treaties. This criticism might have some validity if it were possible for present alliance members to achieve their common security objectives through the United Nations, but this is not possible. The United Nations is essentially a continuing conference of eighty-one legally sovereign states. It has no independent existence or power apart from the existence and power of its member states. It is not a repository of power, but an instrument which is used, abused or brushed aside in the struggle of power and purpose among nation-states. The decisions of war and peace rest with the governments of soveriegn states, especially with the governments of the two superpowers. The United Nations, by its very nature, cannot transcend but must reflect the bipolar power struggle of our time.[6]

Other critics insist that the free-world alliance policy has increased international tension and the possibility of war. Alliances may increase tension, but this is not necessarily bad. Western alliances also increase the bargaining power of the free world and its power to deter Soviet aggression. It is not possible to negotiate with the Soviet Union, Red China or any other power from a position of weakness. Most students of international politics, at least on this side of the Iron Curtain, believe that the existence of a strong free-world coalition forced the Soviet Union and China to call a halt to the Korean War and finally, in 1955, forced the Soviets to agree to an Austrian peace treaty.

Our grand strategy in the Cold War, of which our alliances are a vital part, must be judged in terms of our three-fold objective to prevent the Communist bloc from nibbling us to death, to prevent both "brushfires" and a nuclear war, and, failing to prevent hostilities, to have a sufficiently powerful and diversified military arsenal to win either "brushfires" or a thermonuclear war. It would appear that our alliance policy has served these objectives well. NATO has doubtless been far more significant than our Asian pacts, but the deterrent effect of even a loosely-knit alliance should not be underestimated. Most of our citizens would agree with a statement made by James Reston on Christmas Day, 1955: "Of the 166 million Americans 2.9 million are serving in the Armed Forces . . . and over one million Americans are serving in sixty-three countries overseas, which is probably the main reason why there is as much peace in the world this Christmas as there is." [7]

The break between the United States and her two historic allies, Britain and France, during the Suez crisis of 1956, is a vivid illustration of how difficult it is to manage alliances and keep them in good repair. Usually alliances can exist as viable forces only so long as the major members recognize a serious and common threat. Even when common objectives and mutual dependence are recognized, the members of the alliance must submit to certain disciplines if the united effort is to succeed. One of these disciplines is prior consultation with other members on problems of mutual concern. A formal treaty is no guarantee that such consultation will take place. Secretary Dulles and President Eisenhower were greatly displeased because the British and French acted in the Suez crisis without prior consultation. Observers on both sides of the Atlantic said that Mr. Dulles was "just getting back some of his own medicine." In the spring of 1946, when Mr. Dulles suggested that NATO be "strengthened" by an increase of its jurisdiction in economic and social matters, most European diplomats felt that he was evading the central problem which was facing the alliance. Next to the Soviet "peace offensive" and the downgrading of Stalin which were then current, these diplomats said in private that the greatest obstacle to a more effective NATO was Mr. Dulles' habit of announcing American policies which vitally affected the interests of other partners in the alliance without prior consultation and sometimes even without prior information. Mr. Dulles' habit of occasionally failing to take our allies into confidence dates back to 1953. During 1953 and the first half of 1954, according to one study, the British Government was placed on the defensive before Parliament on eleven different occasions because the United States government announced policies or proposals intimately involving Britain without full prior consultation. We are not suggesting that Britain and France were retaliating for diplomatic snubs they had suffered in the past, because the reasons underlying their unilateral action in the Suez crisis are far more complex and, certainly, more worthy than that. Nor are we attempting to justify British and French policy. We are merely saying that even the strongest alliances are difficult to maintain.

No amount of structural manipulation within an alliance can make up for a lack of diplomatic courtesy and integrity. An *informal coalition* resting upon a mutual recognition of common interests and in which the member states consult one another on mutual problems is far more effective than a *formal alliance* in which member states are constantly making unilateral policy announcements and "agonizing reappraisals." A genuine partnership of nations can have a wholesome and restraining influence on any member of the alliance who might be tempted to embark on an unwise or reckless adventure. It does not require much imagination to anticipate what might happen in Formosa and South Korea if Chiang Kai-shek and President Rhee were not restrained by our alliance with these countries located so precariously on the periphery of Communist China. At its best an alliance provides an atmosphere conducive to mutual criticism in which the wisdom, experience and interests of each participating country are shared for the benefit of all. At worst it is an empty shell which may deceive some of its members, but is not likely to deceive its enemies.

Alliance policies are not necessarily wiser than unilateral policies, nor are they morally superior. There is nothing inherently virtuous about acting in concert. A band of thieves is a mutual enterprise. There are bad alliance policies and good unilateral policies. All foreign policies must ultimately be judged by their intention and their effect upon persons at home and abroad. The network of American-led alliances seems to have contributed to international peace and stability as well as to American security.

A military alliance, like all military power, is primarily a protective shield. There is nothing creative about military defense as such. An alliance may stop the spread of injustice and tyranny, but it cannot create freedom, justice or community. An alliance is not a substitute for a sound national military establishment within the United States. Nor is it a substitute for diplomatic, economic or psychological foreign policy measures. Our alliance policy is a part of our over-all foreign policy and must contribute to the objectives of that policy. Alliances must be constantly reviewed to see if they are in fact serving their purpose in the ever-changing international situation.

"Massive Retaliation" vs. "Graduated Deterrence"

The decision of Great Britain to put a greater percentage of her defense eggs in the nuclear basket, and of the Soviet Union to organize a new "rocket force" on a par with its army, navy and air force, both announced in April 1947, focus attention on a problem which has been debated in the United States ever since the end of World War II. Two competing conceptions of our over-all military strategy have been vying for ascendency in political and military circles in Washington. The debate is not between mutually-exclusive alternatives, but between two emphases within a generally accepted set of common strategic assumptions. Both sides agree that we should have a "balanced arsenal of weapons," but they cannot agree on what a *balanced* arsenal consists of. The outcome of this debate, of which large sectors of the American public are unaware, may have a significant political and moral effect on the character of our alliances, the nature of our military establishment, and the character of any future war. It may even determine whether or not there is to be a nuclear holocaust.

One strategic conception in this debate can be characterized by the term "massive retaliation," which Secretary Dulles used to describe his policy of instant and massive atomic retaliation at points of our own choosing in the event of a serious threat to our national security. This policy gives a high priority to strategic atomic and nuclear weapons over conventional arms or tactical atomic weapons. It emphasizes the necessity of a Strategic Air Command capable of delivering nuclear weapons to large strategic targets, such as air fields and cities, anywhere in the world. It is difficult to ascertain whether Mr. Dulles actually regards "massive retaliation" as a substantial departure from the policies followed since 1947, or whether he felt compelled to promote certain "catch words" to gain favor with the economy-minded political leaders who want "a bigger bang for a buck."

The doctrine of "massive retaliation," or primary reliance on nuclear firepower and means of delivery, has been highly criticized by students of foreign policy in this country and abroad. Paul H. Nitze, a former director of the State Department Policy Planning Staff, has been one of the most vocal critics. He and other students of the problem offer as an alternative to "massive retaliation" a military strategy based upon "graduated deterrence." [8] "Graduated deterrence" insists upon the necessity of including in our arsenal conventional arms, tactical atomic firepower, and strategic nuclear weapons, giving relatively equal priority to each category. Such an arsenal would have the flexibility necessary to meet successfully all kinds of attacks which threaten our security from small "brushfires" to an all-out nuclear assault. It would also have the capability of restoring the pre-attack situation with the minimum of effort and destruction. Thus, if the Soviet Union moved against Iran or Turkey, the United States would not drop H-bombs on Moscow or any other Soviet city. Instead, we would, if possible, meet the attack locally, perhaps using tactical atomic weapons in conjunction with conventional arms. If this effort were not successful the United States would attempt to destroy the air fields from which a general Soviet attack could be launched. Nuclear weapons would not be used against Soviet population centers unless she started to drop such weapons on Teheran, Istanbul, London or New York.

A strategic policy of "graduated deterrence" has several advantages over a policy of "massive retaliation." Tailoring the defense to fit the attack tends to localize the conflict and reduce the destruction on both sides. This in turn tends to reduce the likelihood of a general nuclear war. Even in the event of nuclear war, the greater flexibility of a balanced arsenal would be more capable of limiting the destruction to the minimum required to restore the pre-attack situation. "Graduated deterrence" has one major disadvantage—

it costs more. More men and more arms of every type are required to gain sufficient power and flexibility to meet effectively any situation from a "brushfire" to a total nuclear attack. Since this is more expensive than primary reliance on "push-button" weapons, the basic strategic decision of the United States may be determined largely by economic considerations as in the case of Britain, and this decision may be made in the near future if it has not already been made. A series of recent decisions has seemed to indicate an increasing reliance on rockets and other weapons equipped with nuclear warheads. On April 12, 1957, for example, our government announced that it would furnish three new missiles—the Honest John and Matador ground-to-ground missiles, and the Nike ground-to-air missile—to our NATO allies, but without nuclear warheads. The supplying of nuclear components is at present forbidden by Congress. Further, by midsummer 1957 our four-billion-dollar ballistic missile development program had already reached its test-flight phase. In addition to economy, another factor which may support the growing reliance on nuclear weapons is the increasing precision and controllability of some of the new devices.

The Big Four Summit meeting in July 1955, at which Soviet and American leaders appear to have acknowledged that resort to general thermonuclear war would be irrational, except under the most extreme provocation, has tended to point up the desirability of "graduated deterrence." The uneasy "nuclear stalemate" has not ended the Cold War, or the necessity of maintaining an atomic and conventional arms balance between the two blocs. Rather, it has somewhat untied the hands of the Kremlin to employ less-than-atomic means to achieve its foreign policy objectives, without fear of nuclear reprisal. This may mean that the Soviet will furnish other small nations with arms as in the case of Egypt; or even stimulate occasional "brushfires" such as the one in Indo-China. The West must prepare for any eventuality. A sound foreign policy for the United States in this era of "competitive coexistence" should include military co-operation with our free-world allies, a balanced arsenal of weapons, and the strengthening of our diplomatic, psychological and economic efforts, especially in those areas where Soviet penetration is already most advanced or most likely.

Coexistence and Armament Control

The level of armament in the opposing camps of the present bipolar struggle is chiefly a reflection of the degree of hostility which exists between them. The basic cause of this hostility is the Soviet Union's policy of political, territorial and ideological expansion and the means she employs to further her objectives. The chances for a substantial cut in defense budgets in the free world appear to be slight as long as the Soviets actively pursue their goal of world domination by force and subversion. In spite of great difficulties, however, the West should continue to work for an effective system of armament control and limitation based upon an enforceable inspection system. New and unexpected opportunities for some progress in this direction may be presented to the world as a result of internal changes within the Soviet empire. We should be alert to such possibilities. It would be politically suicidal and morally indefensible for the United States to diminish her arms drastically or to destroy her stockpile of atomic and nuclear weapons merely on the basis of a promise that the

Soviet Union would do the same. Conversely, we have no right to ask the Soviets to reduce their arms unless they have an opportunity to verify our promise to reduce ours.

Efforts to control the dangers from radioactive fallout from nuclear tests should be constantly explored. Experimental tests undertaken by the United States should employ all the known safeguards for controlling dangerous radioactivity.

President Eisenhower has said, "there is no alternative to peace," and Reinhold Niebuhr adds, "but there are alternative kinds of peace." National security means little if we do not have a nation fully worthy of defense. Even in this period of cold war, there are many things which can be done to make our country more worthy of the sacrifices of blood and treasure we as the leader of the free-world coalition have already made and will be called upon to make in the future.

CHAPTER THREE

*Foreign policies demand scarcely any of those quali-
ties which are peculiar to a democracy; they require,
on the contrary, the perfect use of almost all those in
which it is deficient. . . . [A democracy] cannot combine its measures with secrecy or await their consequences with patience.*

ALEXIS DE TOCQUEVILLE, 1835

THE DILEMMA OF DEMOCRATIC DIPLOMACY

In a calculated attempt to expel the United States,
Britain and France from their strategic position behind the Iron Curtain in East Germany, the Soviet
Union on June 24, 1948, imposed a blockade against
all surface traffic from West Germany to Berlin. The
blockade clearly violated the Four-Power agreements
giving the Western powers "free access by air, road
and rail" to their respective occupation sectors in the
former German capital. The United States and Britain
responded to this serious political crisis by initiating
a gigantic airlift to supply their garrisons, the French
garrison and 2,500,000 residents of Berlin with food
and fuel. After almost a year of intense diplomatic
negotiation, and some two hundred thousand airlift
flights later, the Soviets called off the blockade. For
political and economic reasons the Western powers
continued the airlift, but in substantially reduced volume, until October 1, 1949. By that date a total of
277,264 flights had brought to Berlin 2,343,301 tons
of supplies.

The ending the Berlin blockade without resorting to war was one of the greatest diplomatic victories of the West since the end of World War II. This victory is a tribute to diplomacy—not to diplomacy as an isolated method, but to diplomacy as *one* of the indispensable instruments of a sound and effective foreign policy. In the Berlin crisis Western diplomacy was supported by the determination to stay in Berlin, so dramatically demonstrated by the airlift, as well as by the power of the West in terms of the atomic bomb, American military aid to Greece and Turkey, the Marshall Plan, and the newly-signed North Atlantic Treaty. When the United States negotiated with the Soviet Union on the Berlin situation, she negotiated from a position of strength. Diplomacy is only one instrument of foreign policy along with other instruments—military, economic and psychological— however, it is closely intertwined with and dependent upon the other instruments. An effective diplomacy must always take into account and make use of political, military, economic and psychological factors.

What Is Diplomacy?

The word *diplomacy* is often used as a synonym for foreign policy—we speak, for example, of the history of American diplomacy. More precisely diplomacy refers to the *conduct* of foreign policy as opposed to the formulation of foreign policy. Used in this more restricted sense diplomacy embraces the techniques of representation, persuasion, negotiation and pressure. In this chapter and throughout the present work the word diplomacy is used in the more precise sense with particular emphasis on its central characteristic—*negotiation*. In fact, negotiation can be said to include representation, persuasion, pressure, manipulation and bargaining. Diplomacy consists of *political* representation abroad or in any official contact with a foreign government, as opposed to economic, cultural or informational forms of representation. Diplomatic negotiation, supported by military, economic and psychological measures, is the major instrument used by governments in the conduct of their foreign relations.

The ultimate objective of diplomacy is the same as that of foreign policy generally—to serve the national purpose and the more specific interests which flow from this purpose. The immediate objective of diplomacy is to pursue the goals of foreign policy successfully and at the least cost. Today, with the ominous threat of nuclear war hanging over mankind, the central task of international diplomacy is to prevent or limit military action by mitigating and minimizing conflicts between nations. Under these circumstances a diplomacy which ends in war has failed.

Constant negotiation among the governments of sovereign states is inevitable for precisely the same reason that negotiation within every social group from the family to a giant corporation is inevitable. In every human group there are mutual interests which can be protected and advanced by common agreements reached through negotiation. In every group there are also conflicts of interests which must be accommodated through negotiation if the group is to survive. Diplomatic negotiation deals with the mutuality of interests among nations as well as the conflicts of interest between them. The conflicts of interest among states would have little or no possibility of being mitigated if it were not for the underlying common interests which bind them together in spite of their differences.

The mutual national interests which are harmonized through diplomatic negotiation include the allocation of short-wave radio frequencies, international post and communication, the amenities and immunities of diplomats, and hundreds of other technical problems whose solution benefits all the nations subscribing to the international agreements covering such matters. These technical problems, as long as they remain technical, cause little friction in international affairs, but they require quiet but constant diplomatic attention. The relatively high degree of international harmony on this technical level has little if any impact on the resolution of the basic political conflicts between nations.

Diplomacy is not really tested until it is tested in the political arena. The crucial diplomatic problem of our day has to do with the profound differences which divide the Soviet world from the free world. This is primarily a political and moral problem and only secondarily a technical problem. It is a thousand times more difficult to deal with the politically-motivated jamming of Voice of America broadcasts in the Soviet Union than it is to deal with the technical problem of allocating radio frequencies, even among hostile states.

Preconditions of Diplomatic Negotiation

Since diplomacy is conducted in behalf of a nation state, it must serve the purposes and interests of the state and, if possible, the larger interests of international peace and security. No morally responsible diplomat may bargain away the national interests of his country in order to achieve a settlement, even if his refusal to do so may invite war or the risk of war. Even less may a responsible statesman bargain away the interests of an ally or neutral power. In negotiating with Hitler, admittedly a rather one-sided business, the Quislings bargained away the interests of their own countries and Prime Minister Chamberlain sold the interests of Czechoslovakia for an empty promise.

To be effective, diplomacy must be supported by adequate national power. No diplomat can constantly overplay his hand and get away with it. International politics is the struggle of power and purpose; any nation which seeks objectives completely incommensurate with its capabilities is doomed to disappointment. Squirrels who try to behave like elephants are both laughable and pathetic.[1]

Successful negotiation is an art which places heavy demands upon the wisdom, sensitivity, strategic skill and patience of the statesmen to whom it is entrusted. Apart from the personal skills of the diplomatist and his recognition that diplomacy must serve the national interest and be based upon adequate power, there are three fundamental preconditions for effective negotiation.

First, diplomatic negotiation can be effective only when both states involved in a controversy recognize the right of the other state to exist, or at least recognize the fact that the other state does exist. When Soviet Party Chief Krushchev said in 1956, "We will bury you yet," he meant that, according to the Communist world view, the United States as the leader of the "Capitalist bloc" did not have a moral right to exist. But as a matter of practical politics Mr. Krushchev is less concerned about the moral right of the United States to exist than about the political fact that she does exist, and constitutes the major political barrier to the goals of Soviet imperialism. Therefore, under certain circumstances the Soviet Union is willing to negotiate, trade, bargain, and compromise with her "enemy" with the hope that in the future, perhaps the very near future, history will prove to have been on her side. Contemporary Middle Eastern politics provides another example of this problem. Egypt and other Arab states do not recognize the moral right of Israel to exist and, consequently, do not recognize her legal existence. Therefore the Arab states cannot negotiate with Israel because to them she does not legally exist, however eloquent the evidence of her political evidence may be.

During the past fifty years the problem of diplomacy has been seriously aggravated by the development of national political religions or national "systems of self-righteousness" which tend to create unbridgeable chasms between the "chosen nation" and other nations. Crusading national ideologies, such as Nazism and Communism, turn their back on any live-and-let-live scruples in their imperial messianism and regard other nations as targets for conquest through subversion or war. The slogan of 1938 and 1939, "You can't do business with Hitler," expressed an important truth, for after the point of no return had been reached, "negotiation" with Hitler became a mockery. Intense political religions not only preclude negotiation; they often lead to war. William Graham Sumner once said, "If you want war, nourish a doctrine." [2]

It is easy for us to see how national systems of self-righteousness such as Fascism, Nazism and Communism have made negotiation almost impossible when these systems were supported by dominant power. It is more difficult to see how certain attitudes in the United States point ominously in the same direction. A widespread attitude toward Communist China both in the general public and in official circles might be regarded as a form of national self-righteousness or moralism. According to this view we refuse to recognize China's legal existence because we are unwilling to grant her a moral right to exist. Fortunately, our practice is not wholly consistent in this matter. While we do not acknowledge the People's Republic of China as a legal entity, by our negotiation for the release of American prisoners in China we do recognize her as a political reality. As of August 1957 our State Department had not validated the passports of American newsmen who sought to enter Red China. This attitude toward China is all the more confusing when we note the ease with which reporters and other American citizens get permission from the State Department to visit the Soviet Union, whose domestic and foreign policies also fall under our moral disapproval. We can be grateful that this principle of basing legal recognition on moral approval is honored more in the breach than in the observance.

National self-righteousness, whether of a mild or a severe variety, always makes it more difficult to negotiate with nations "beyond the pale," and occasionally even poisons relations with trusted allies. In early 1957, for example, President Eisenhower refused to invite Sir Anthony Eden, then British Prime Minister, to visit him in Washington when Sir Anthony was in Jamaica, on the ground that such a visit would give the impression that the United States approved of Britian's invasion of Egypt.[3]

Second, diplomatic negotiation can be effective only when each state is willing to take into account the interest of its antagonist and of other nations. When a nation has a "decent respect for the opinions of mankind" and recognizes that other nations have legitimate interests, including the right to exist, it can negotiate with other powers, even smaller ones, without violating their moral or political integrity.

Carl Sandburg observed that the "cockroach is always wrong when it argues with the chicken," but fortunately the moral capacity of some nations, at least on occasion, exceeds that of chickens. Few Norwegians, for example, would hold that the powerful United States forced Norway to join NATO against her will. And few Panamanians would regard the recent United States-Panama agreements on the future of the Canal as big-power dominations.

The prospects for the successful diplomatic adjustment of conflicting interests are enhanced if both sides have the wisdom and prudence to see their differences within the larger context of their mutual interests. In fact, the settlement of conflicting national interests is not possible without the recognition of an underlying mutuality of interests. This fact is easy to grasp when we are considering relations between friendly nations such as Britain and the United States. It is more difficult to comprehend when we consider relations between hostile nations. We sometimes hear it said that the United States has nothing in common with the Soviet Union. This is not true, because the Soviets and the Americans have a profound mutual interest in avoiding all-out nuclear war. Recognizing this powerful common interest, each side in the Cold War should be able to face the very real conflicts of interest which divide us with a greater sense of proportion and perspective. A recognition of common interests does not eliminate conflict, but it does help to create an atmosphere in which conflict can be grappled with realistically and perhaps imaginatively.

Third, diplomatic negotiation can be effective only when both sides are willing to compromise on less-than-vital issues. If politics is the art of compromise, political ethics is concerned with achieving the least immoral compromise possible. The advocates of a political ethic based directly upon absolute moral principles understand neither the limits of politics nor the Biblical recognition of the weaknesses and moral ambiguity of man. Compromise in international politics is inevitable. The goal of a sound and morally-responsible diplomat is to achieve compromises which respect the legitimate interests of his own government and the government with which he is negotiating.

Since a diplomat engaged in genuine negotiation can never fully achieve all the goals of his country, he must at the outset of the negotiation have made a distinction in his mind between the vital and the less-than-vital interests of his government. Vital interests, by definition, cannot be surrendered. When a statesman identifies an interest as vital, he means that his country cannot relinquish this interest without a fight. The preservation of an independent South Korea oriented toward the West was a vital interest of the United States; therefore, we fought to maintain it. Consequently, most of the bargaining and "horse trading" in international diplomacy involves less-than-vital interests because such interests are negotiable. Diplomats surrender the less-than-vital interests of their country so that they will not have to surrender the vital ones. The United States surrendered its interest in a Western-allied Austria and settled for an independent and neutral Austria in 1955 because she had a *negative* vital interest in the continued Soviet domination of eastern Austria. The Soviet Union in like manner surrendered her interest in a Soviet-allied Austria in order to prevent Austria or a part of Austria from becoming allied militarily with the West.

The most difficult problems of diplomacy have to do with conflicting vital interests. Germany provides a good example. Both the Soviet Union and the West want a united Germany allied with their side. Each is determined to keep the other from achieving this objective. Consequently we have two Germanys, one allied with the East and the other with the West. The Germans themselves want to be politically united, but not under Soviet domination. Some Germans want unity even if it means Austrian-like neutrality. The Soviets fear that a united and free Germany would ally itself to the West. The United States fears that a united and unarmed Germany would be a target for Soviet penetration and subversion. There is no easy solution. Conceivably this impasse could be resolved, or at least accommodated, by grappling with it in the larger context of a general European or world-wide settlement which would take into account many interests of each side in the Cold War. Such an accomplishment, if it could be realized, would involve a recognition on both sides of significant common interests which transcend the conflicting interests, and a manipulation of less-than-vital interests in such a way that the nature and claim of the vital interests would be transformed to the point at which they are negotiable. If there is to be a substantial relaxation in the Cold War, bold and creative diplomacy of this quality will be required.

The Deprecation and Decline of Traditional Diplomacy

The traditional diplomacy of the three centuries prior to 1900, says Kenneth W. Thompson, was carried on by a "body of aristocratic sovereigns who spoke the same language, shared common cultural values, were bound by family ties, and, in a word, were members of the same club. Moreover, these rulers were served by diplomats and soldiers whose sense of national or dynastic loyalty was never so great as to exclude" possible employment with a different sovereign. Mr. Thompson continues: "The respect and dependence members of this aristocratic elite felt for one another led them to observe the rules of the game. Beyond this their goals were simple and limited. They might seek a piece of territory, a bit of glory or greater power and prestige. But the whole world was not their oyster and they accepted the fact that they were partners in an international order that 'gentlemen' were pledged to preserve."[4] These classical diplomats did their work behind closed doors, responsive to their sovereign's wishes and restrained by their loyalty to common supra-national values, but with little thought for the opinions of the common people. "In the days of the old diplomacy," says Sir Harold Nicolson, "it would have been an act of unthinkable vulgarity to appeal to the common people upon any issue of international policy." The object of the traditional diplomatists, says Hans J. Morgenthau, was not to avoid war "but to bring it about at the most propitious moment."

With the coming of the industrial revolution, the ideas of popular sovereignty, and the rise of modern democratic states, the old unifying fabric of European civilization was rent, its moral values shattered, and its political institutions fragmented. Domestic and international politics became responsive to the popular will, and diplomacy was forced to adjust to the demands of liberal democracy.

The old diplomacy was discredited along with the old order. Woodrow Wilson and other critics of traditional diplomacy said it was immoral, undemocractic and led to war. It was undemocratic and immoral because it was conducted in secret and thus did not give "the people" a voice in the grave issues of war and peace. The Old World diplomats were regarded as conniving and intriguing schemers whose evil ways almost always led to military conflict. World War I was regarded as the final foul fruit of the old autocratic and aristocratic diplomacy.

With the deprecation of the old diplomacy came a clarion call for a new and democratic diplomacy. Only when the people with their inherent wisdom and virtue took charge of international affairs would there be lasting peace. Although scholars still disagree on how Wilsonian Wilson really was, it would appear that he did regard secrecy as a major, if not the major, evil in traditional diplomacy. In the first of his famous Fourteen Points he called for "open covenants openly arrived at" and said that "diplomacy should proceed always frankly and in the public view." In 1919 when Wilson left for the Paris Peace Conference he promised to conduct no secret negotiations and to sign no secret treaties. He kept his latter promise scrupulously, but quickly broke the former one, according to Sir Harold Nicolson, a British diplomatic historian who attended the Paris Conference. Sir Harold relates this incident:

"I remember on one occasion [at the Paris Conference] being summoned to what was called 'The Council of Three.' After passing through successive police barriers that guarded the President's private house, I approached the inner holy of holies, at the door of which stood a sturdy marine grasping a rifle in his hand. On entering the room I found Lloyd George seated in one armchair, M. Clemenceau seated in another armchair, and the President kneeling on the floor and peering at an enormous map spread upon the hearth-rug. Outside the window . . . another marine paced up and down with his bayonet fixed. 'This,' I thought to myself, 'is what is called arriving at a covenant openly.' "[5]

This incident is recalled not to reflect on Wilson's

integrity, but to illustrate how a morally-responsible statesman can rise above his political theory in order to make an impact upon political reality. After a few days in Paris Wilson knew that nothing of value could be accomplished if negotiations had to be conducted in the "public view." It is difficult to understand why he carried any such illusions to Paris in the first place, in light of the fact that months before he had clarified his original statement in these words: "When I pronounced for open diplomacy, I meant not that there should be no private discussions of delicate matters, but that no secret agreements should be entered upon, and that all international relations, when fixed, should be open, above-board, and explicit." [6]

Negotiation must always be conducted in private because of the nature of negotiation itself. Negotiation is concerned with settling conflicts between individual, group or national egos. Privacy is a basic prerequisite for transforming egos and interests into a working compromise. Apparently some of Wilson's more ardent followers believed that the realm of international politics was somehow exempted from the elementary contingencies and requirements of all other forms of human association.

The New Diplomacy, American Style

After World War I, America adopted the new diplomacy of democracy and turned its back on the old diplomacy of secrecy and intrigue. In fact, most Americans believed that our country had never been tainted with the Old World diplomacy. The postwar advocates of democratic diplomacy insisted upon open negotiation and public participation, although it was never clear in what way the public could actually participate. They also emphasized multilateral rather than bilateral negotiation. The new diplomacy was to be conducted by parliament-like international bodies such as the League of Nations, where negotiation could be public, multilateral and democratic at the same time. Through such international "peace machinery" the natural wisdom and moral sense of the people would replace the evil designs of the professional diplomats and the world would have peace at last.

The insistence on the moral superiority of multilateral negotiation in a parliament-like setting was sometimes supported by the belief that smaller nations had a virtue and a wisdom which was denied the great powers. Today the idea of giving the smaller powers a "greater voice" in the United Nations Assembly appears to be an expression of the same belief. Few smaller powers claim superior virtue or wisdom, but some citizens of powerful states, perhaps out of a sense of guilt for the power their country has acquired, seem to believe they do. Political wisdom and moral insight may not be commensurate with the power a nation has, but moral responsibility certainly is. Consequently the great powers should have a greater voice than the smaller powers at the United Nations and in world politics generally. Nations, like men, have a moral responsibility commensurate with their gifts.

Between the two World Wars the major forum for the new diplomacy was the League of Nations, where both public and multilateral negotiation, or what appeared to be negotiation, could flourish. Since 1945 the major forums have been the United Nations and a series of highly-publicized international conferences among heads of state or foreign ministers. These high-level meetings should be distinguished from international consultations of experts which enjoy little publicity and do not fall within the category of "public diplomacy." The value of this kind of confidential consultation and negotiation among experts has not been questioned.

The new diplomacy, because of the strong support it receives in the United States, is sometimes known as "American diplomacy." In the past five or more years this "conference diplomacy," "parliamentary diplomacy," "fish-bowl diplomacy," "glass-house diplomacy," or "propaganda diplomacy," as it has been variously characterized, has been the subject of an increasing stream of criticism from scholars, statesmen and journalists.

Professor Morgenthau believes that "diplomacy by parliamentary procedures" should be eliminated because these procedures tend to "aggravate rather than to mitigate international conflicts." Walter Lippmann urges Western governments to "liberate themselves from the compulsion to go on trying to do business in a series of public conferences." C. L. Sulzberger says "it is surely time that normal customs of diplomacy be resumed. The postwar trend toward diplomacy by conference, diplomacy by loudspeaker and diplomacy by insult has been hysterical." Even United Nations Secretary General Dag Hammarskjold has emphasized the value of "quiet diplomacy" as "a complement to the conference diplomacy of public debates," observing that the latter contains "an aspect of propaganda and an element of rigidity which may be harmful to sound negotiation." Sir Winston Churchill wanted the "summit" meeting of the Big Four to be small, informal and free from publicity. President Eisenhower had a somewhat different view, although he has on at least one occasion openly supported secret negotiations. In August

1954, Mr. Eisenhower said: "It is obvious that much of the diplomatic work, particularly those efforts that are classed as preparatory toward the reaching of agreements, be conducted in confidence . . . premature disclosures of positions and arguments could very well bar the attainment of any reasonable solution."

Only a small portion of the real business at the United Nations or at recent international conferences is actually conducted "in the public view." Just as was the case at the Paris Conference in 1919, the basic agreements are hammered out in secret, although many American citizens believed that significant negotiation is taking place in public. Strictly speaking, "public negotiation" is a contradiction in terms. Nevertheless, since many activities at the United Nations and international conferences are open to immediate public scrutiny, and since "public diplomacy" does exist in theory and practice, it may be useful to summarize eight of its interrelated weaknesses as seen by its critics. These weaknesses are really roadblocks to effective diplomatic negotiation.

1. Public diplomacy subjects the diplomat to the shifting moods and emotions of a public which cannot fully understand the complexity and delicacy of the problems under discussion. The public, with the aid of political or journalistic slogan-makers, tends to become emotionally attached to "catch phrases" which may bear little relation to the real issues involved. Editors, members of Congress and leaders of civic and religious groups are sometimes tempted to think of themselves as having some special competence in the technical matters under consideration by professional diplomats.

2. Public diplomacy subjects the diplomat to the pressure of various sub-national groups which are likely to have a clearer understanding of their own

special interests than of the national interest. Business, labor, women's, ethnic, veterans', professional and church groups are in a position to put pressure on the negotiator directly or through Congress. The advice of these groups on complex issues is usually too poorly informed or too narrowly conceived to be relevant.[7]

3. Public diplomacy tends to increase the role of Congress in foreign policy at the expense of the Executive Branch. Congressional inroads on the President's Constitutional powers to conduct foreign relations have posed a serious threat since 1950. This problem has probably been aggravated by United States participation in United Nations and conference diplomacy.[7a]

4. Public diplomacy encourages propaganda speeches rather than a genuine effort to compromise the conflicting interests involved. The diplomats are tempted to exploit their "international forum" to gain favor with political and other special-interest pressure groups at home or to influence "peoples" abroad. The temptation to engage in propaganda rather than negotiation is much greater when either or both sides are convinced that no settlement is possible. On a number of occasions both the Soviet Union and the United States assumed that a stalemate would not be broken; consequently, each side used the occasion to get its point of view across to the widest possible audience. This is what happened in response to the Hungarian revolution of 1956 at the United Nations. There was no real negotiation, but there were many resolutions and a great deal of speechmaking. This is not to say that the resolutions were meaningless and the speeches were of no value, but only to suggest that there was no genuine attempt to negotiate on either side because the issue was regarded as closed. There was no serious effort

on the part of the West to challenge Soviet political hegemony in Hungary.

5. Public diplomacy tends to tie the hands of the diplomat. The inescapable compromises of negotiation must be constantly and speedily justified to the various publics and pressure groups back home. Once a diplomat has taken a position it is difficult and almost impossible for him to make the necessary concessions for a viable settlement. This makes for rigidity and dries up any liquid assets he may have had at the outset of the talks.

6. Public diplomacy tends to be hurried, and thus leads to hasty improvisations or empty formulas. It is hurried because there are a specified number of items on the agenda which must be "dealt with" by a specified date. Pressed by lack of time and preoccupied with what the people back home may think, the harried diplomats often issue meaningless communiqués in order not to disappoint their constituencies. They are tempted to become more interested in public relations than in public responsibility. The joint British-American statement at the close of the Bermuda conference between Prime Minister Macmillan and President Eisenhower in March 1957, is an example of this problem.

7. Public diplomacy tends to create unwarranted and unrealistic expectations in large segments of the public. When these expectations are unfulfilled, the public mood often shifts from optimism to pessimism or even to cynicism. The "failure" of an international conference tends to cast discredit not only upon the conference but upon the diplomatic process itself. The people become fed up with "polite talk" and "perfumed notes," to use Senator McCarthy's phrase, and demand "action," which may mean anything from "getting tough" to launching a preventive war. The Eisenhower Administration, segments of the press, and

some church leaders must share the blame for the psychological backwash which resulted from their overselling the Big Four Summit Conference in 1955.

8. Public diplomacy tends to undercut the solid, steady and quiet work of ambassadors and other members of the diplomatic corps. Effective diplomacy must be continuous, confidential and patient. It must be conducted by men who by reason of training or experience are highly qualified. Public diplomacy tends to be hasty, spasmodic and public-relations conscious. Direct negotiation between heads of state or foreign ministers has certain inherent weaknesses. Sir Harold Nicolson says: "A minister who flies to a foreign capital to undertake negotiation is inevitably short of time, ill equipped in technical knowledge, subjected to great publicity and inclined to conclude some vague and meaningless agreement rather than to return empty-handed to his home. More misery has been caused to mankind by the hurried drafting of imprecise or meaningless documents than by all the alleged machinations of the cunning diplomatist. Thus I should, whenever feasible, leave it to the professional to do his job quietly and without fuss." [8] One need not agree fully with Nicolson to see the dangers in the "personal diplomacy" of Secretary Dulles, who seems to regard himself as the indispensable "troubleshooter" for the West at assorted centers of strife around the globe. On April 13, 1957, the *New York Times* reported that Mr. Dulles had flown 329,058 miles in foreign missions since he took office in January 1953. There are, of course, occasional international conferences which the Secretary of State by treaty or custom is required to attend. However, Walter Lippmann says Dulles' "peculiar conception of his office . . . requires him not only to make and direct foreign policy but also in the big matters to administer it personally. This has meant his being away from

his office so much of the time that it has been impossible for him to be in intimate touch with the conduct of foreign policy." [9]

A New Look at the Old Diplomacy

The rising chorus of criticism against the new diplomacy has stimulated a new interest in the virtues of the old diplomacy. Traditional diplomacy at its best, says Nicolson, "was courteous and dignified; it was continuous and gradual; it attached importance to knowledge and experience; it took account of the realities of existing power; and it defined good faith, lucidity, and precision as the qualities essential to any sound negotiation." [10]

But traditional diplomacy did not always operate at its best. And the twentieth century is not the seventeenth or the eighteenth century. Change in the conduct of foreign relations was inevitable and desirable. There were two vices of the old diplomacy, each closely related to one of its central virtues, confidential negotiation. One vice was the habit among some diplomats of failing to divulge their commitments to those who had a right to know what agreements had been made, and the other was the failure to take fully into account the real interests of the whole nation they were sworn to serve. The first failure was the failure of men, not of a system. The second failure was the failure of the prevailing political institutions and ethics of the times, and not a failure of diplomacy itself. In those days international politics was a game of kings; the effect of this game upon the great mass of their subjects was not a primary consideration. The concepts of popular sovereignty and parliamentary democracy changed all this.

Nevertheless, if the old diplomacy at its best was as Nicolson describes it, contemporary American diplomacy can learn a great deal from it. Of all the virtues of traditional diplomacy—courtesy, dignity, integrity, realism, patience and confidentiality—the virtue of confidentiality is perhaps the one that is most neglected today in American practice. Everyone, of course, believes in Wilson's "open covenant." The basic foreign policy of a democratic state should not, and indeed cannot, be kept secret. No government of a free country has a right to obligate its citizens to treaties, alliances or other commitments without the full knowledge and consent of their legislatures, except, of course, for the temporary withholding of certain wartime agreements which must not be revealed to the enemy. But present-day advocates of traditional diplomatic methods agree that "open covenants" should be unopenly arrived at. Contemporary American diplomacy would profit also from a greater share of "old-fashioned" virtues such as courtesy, integrity and realism.

In a very real sense, there has not been an *old* diplomacy and a *new* diplomacy, but only one diplomacy. The so-called new diplomacy is often not really diplomacy at all, but a conscious or unconscious effort to escape diplomacy. Many people today regard the United Nations, for example, as a substitute for the hard realities of international politics. These people do not realize that while the new diplomacy is being pursued at the United Nations and at international conferences, the old diplomacy is at work at the same time, quietly operating behind the scenes away from the glare of publicity. It it also in operation through its traditional channels, the chancelleries of the world, doing to a greater or lesser degree what it has always done. Diplomacy is the art of dealing with conflicts of interest through quiet and confidential negotiation. Its nature is determined by the nature of politics and the requirements of all human association, and cannot be changed to conform to current fashions without subverting its central contribution to a sound and morally-responsible foreign policy.

At best, the new diplomacy has reminded democratic statesmen to take fully into account the interests of the public they serve. At worst, it has distracted our attention from the realities of international politics, weakened the structures and practices of genuine diplomacy, and undermined public confidence in sound diplomatic practices.

Regardless of what one's views may be on secret diplomacy, it seems clear that our country will be engaging in more and more of it in the immediate future. In 1957 Walter Lippmann observed: "If the United States is . . . to have a hand in the intricate and secret, but crucial, diplomatic game now played by Nasser in Egypt, King Saud in Saudi Arabia, and Nuri in Iraq, the United States has to indulge in the un-American practice of secret diplomacy. . . . The art of secret diplomacy is a special art, and not one that can be learned easily or quickly . . . we are embarked on a kind of diplomacy which is outside the American tradition." [11]

Profile of an Effective Diplomat

Diplomacy is a complex business and a delicate art. It can be effectively conducted only by persons with appropriate training and experience. This includes career Foreign Service men as well as qualified political appointees, although it should be noted in passing that not all political appointments show as much respect for the diplomatic qualifications of the candidates as they do for the size of their contributions to the party campaign chest. Joining in the universal praise of the political appointment of John Hay Whitney in 1957 to the Court of St. James, columnist Joseph Alsop said: "This year most of the diplomatic posts in Europe have been crudely placed on the auction block and sold for cash on the barrelhead." [12]

Diplomacy is morally sound when it is the effective instrument of a morally-sound foreign policy. It is possible to have an effective diplomacy enlisted in the service of a morally-indefensible foreign policy. It is likewise possible to have morally-sound policies sold short by a weak and ineffective diplomacy. The following profile of an effective diplomat is concerned with the conduct of foreign policy and not with the substance of policy.

An effective diplomat recognizes the common interests which underlie the conflicting interests between his state and the state with which he is negotiating, and knows that these mutual interests provide a foundation on which even serious differences can be accommodated.

An effective diplomat makes a clear distinction between the vital and the less-than-vital interests of his government and is willing to surrender less-than-vital interests in order to protect vital ones. He has an attaché case full of negotiable assets. He is firm on vital interests and flexible on secondary matters. He is willing to surrender the shadow of worthless rights for the substance of real advantage.

An effective diplomat relates the conflicting national interests of both sides to the actual and potential power of each side. He knows that neither side can negotiate from weakness.

An effective diplomat has good manners. He must speak from strength, but he need not speak loudly or insultingly.

An effective diplomat is a man of integrity. His word can be relied upon by friend and foe alike. Persons who believe that deceit was the handmaiden of the old diplomacy might well ponder these words from the last public utterance of Talleyrand: "Diplomacy is not a science of stratagem and duplicity."

An effective diplomat consults with friendly governments on problems of mutual concern. He does not announce a decision of great interest to an ally without the courtesy, indeed the obligation, of prior consultation or at least prior information.

An effective diplomat does not negotiate in public. "The day secrecy is abolished," said Jules Cambon of France, "negotiations of any kind will become impossible." Sound negotiation must be continuous and confidential.

An effective diplomat has the courage to pursue sound policies even in the face of opposition at home or abroad as long as he is convinced that these policies are in the national interest and that there is sufficient power to support them.

An effective diplomat must know when to speak and when to remain silent. Consider the misunderstanding, anxiety and explaining away occasioned by unnecessary statements such as "massive retaliation," "agonizing reappraisal," and Goa being a "province" of Portugal. A diplomat must learn to speak with precision on crucial issues or remain silent.

An effective diplomat has the capacity to see how the problem appears to other governments and peoples, including governments which are hostile to his own. This kind of sensitivity not only contributes to a realistic appraisal of the situation, but helps the diplomat to understand more fully the degree of underlying mutuality which exists and which may provide a basis for settlement.

If these are the qualities of an effective diplomat, they are also the qualities of an effective and responsible Secretary of State.[13]

American Diplomacy and the Cold War

The very fact that a growing number of scholars and diplomats in this country and abroad are deeply concerned about the unsatisfactory conduct of American diplomacy since the end of World War II is perhaps the most hopeful augury of better days to come. In the early months of the 1956-1957 Middle Eastern crisis, the Eisenhower Administration, according to most competent observers, placed undue reliance on the United Nations as an instrument of diplomacy. This led some scholars to suggest that our government was reverting to the very kind of parliamentary, multilateral and public diplomacy they had hoped we were growing away from. Although it is still too early to speak with assurance, it would appear that this "let-the-United-Nations-do-it" policy may be only an unhappy interlude in a long-term trend toward increasing appreciation for the essential elements of genuine diplomacy. The world-wide criticism of "letting the United Nations carry the ball" is itself evidence that the new diplomacy, American style, may be losing its hold. And yet it may be a long struggle before we shake off the last vestiges of "public diplomacy."

Perhaps we should place our hope in American

pragmatism which so often triumphs over our slogans. During the periods between the two World
Wars and since 1945, when "public diplomacy" was
at its height in popular acceptance and official statements, the old diplomacy was quietly at work in the
capitals of the world and behind the scenes at international conferences. Our political pragmatism had
transcended our political doctrine, or rather a doctrine
chastened by political necessity and the requirements
of international responsibility had triumphed over a
doctrine based upon nineteenth-century illusions
about the nature of man and of history.

The present phase in the Cold War has placed new
demands upon diplomacy. The "nuclear stalemate,"
the death of Stalin, the resurgence of Germany and
Japan, and the growing reliance of both sides on
ballistic missiles have tended to loosen certain rigidi-
ties which characterized the first postwar decade. This
new phase in the bipolar struggle brings with it new
opportunities and dangers. All countries have a profound mutual interest in avoiding a thermonuclear
holocaust, but the responsibility for honoring this
universal interest falls largely upon the United States
and the Soviet Union. If the two superpowers fully
recognize the dimensions of their common peril they
will be able to see the interests that divide them in a
truer and clearer perspective than they have seen
them in the past decade. Such a perspective will
create a climate conducive to fruitful negotiation.
Perhaps Sir Winston Churchill's words of January 23,
1948, are still valid: "I believe it right to say today
that the best chance of avoiding war is, in accord with
the other Western democracies, to bring matters to a
head with the Soviet government, and by formal
diplomatic processes, with all their privacy and
gravity, to arrive at a lasting settlement. . . . It is
idle to reason or argue with the Communists. It is,

however, possible to deal with them on a fair, realistic basis, and, in my experience, they will keep their bargains as long as it is in their interest to do so, which might, in this grave matter, be a long time. . . . There is certainly enough for the interests of all if such a settlement could be reached. Even this method . . . would not guarantee that war would not come. But I believe it would give the best chance of coming out of it alive." [14]

CHAPTER FOUR

It will not do to say that the United Nations will de-
termine policy, make decisions, and enforce them. The
United Nations is not a supranational entity with a
mind, a will, and power. It is a forum, and no more
than the nations which meet there.

DEAN ACHESON, 1957

THE UNITED NATIONS—
INSTRUMENT OF NATIONAL
POLICY

In a nationwide radio and television address to the American people on February 20, 1957, President Eisenhower declared that the failure of Israel to withdraw her remaining troops from Egyptian soil endangered the "future of the United Nations and the peace of the Middle East." "If the United Nations once admits that international disputes can be settled by using force," he said, "then we will have destroyed the very foundation of the organization, and our best hope of establishing a real world order." The United States is seeking "through the United Nations to end conflict" and "to secure justice under international law."

Mr. Eisenhower's condemnation of Israel for her failure to comply with United Nations resolutions was coupled with praise for Britain and France for respecting "the opinions of mankind as expressed almost unanimously by the eighty nation members of the United Nations General Assembly" and thus making "an immense contribution to world order." The

President also condemned the Soviet Union for "its armed suppression of the people of Hungary," but pointed out that we "are entitled to expect" better behavior from Israel because her people "like those of the United States are imbued with a religious faith and a sense of moral values." He noted that the Soviet Union, "by reason of its size and power and by reason of its veto in the United Nations Security Council, is relatively impervious" to economic or military sanctions.

This Presidential address was a remarkable utterance not only because it was devoted primarily to censuring a friendly nation in the name of international morality or because it made no fewer than fifty-four favorable references to the United Nations, but because it was a transparently eloquent demonstration that the American legalism, moralism, and national self-righteousness which had long troubled our allies and which many morally-sensitive Americans had hoped we were at last beginning to outgrow was still very much with us. The speech bears the unmistakable stamp of Secretary of State Dulles, whose moralistic and legalistic approach to foreign policy has been criticized by religious leaders and scholars ever since he became chairman of the Commission on a Just and Durable Peace of the Federal Council of Churches in 1941.[1] We are concerned in this chapter not primarily with the moralism and self-righteousness of the Eisenhower speech, but rather with its legalistic interpretation of international politics in general and of the United Nations in particular. Legalism, which may be defined as an approach to politics which invests in legal symbols, documents, and structures a power and authority which they do not in fact possess, was the constant handmaiden of American liberal idealism in the interwar period. Mr. Eisenhower's address is abundant evidence that the legalistic approach to international politics has not run its course, if indeed evidence were needed.

Four highly questionable assumptions about the nature of the United Nations seem to underlie the President's address: 1) the United Nations is a supranational entity which has a power and existence independent of the nations which constitute it, 2) the United Nations must be preserved at all cost because it is the world's best hope for peace with justice, 3) the United Nations Charter provides an adequate definition of international morality, and 4) the majority decisions of the United Nations General Assembly are morally and politically right and should be obeyed by the erring governments. Neither the speeches nor the policies of Mr. Eisenhower or Mr. Dulles have been consistently instructed by these legalistic assumptions. Fortunately their actual foreign policies, chastened by prudence and political necessity, have often transcended their legalistic and moralistic slogans. But the fact remains that the slogans are frequently invoked and, alas, as the first months of the 1956-1957 Middle Eastern crisis have shown, sometimes followed.[2] The four assumptions of the President's speech correspond closely to the very misconceptions about the United Nations which have been widespread in the United States ever since the Charter was signed in San Francisco in 1945. For this reason alone they are worth careful examination. Among religious and other organizations devoted to international peace the United Nations has probably been the cause or focus of more confusion and misunderstanding than any other single factor since the end of World War II. This is not the fault of the organization but of the inadequate perspective from which the organization is viewed.

Internationalist and Isolationist Views

On July 28, 1945, by a vote of eighty-nine to two, the United States Senate approved American adherence to the United Nations Charter which had been signed in San Francisco a month before. This overwhelming Senate approval reflected the prevailing sentiment in the country. Three days before the Senate acted, a Gallup poll found sixty-six per cent of the American people favorable to the Charter, three per cent unfavorable, and thirty-one per cent undecided.

If the American people were virtually united in supporting their Government's participation in the United Nations, they were divided on how effective they expected the new organization to be in its primary task of preventing war. On the eve of the San Francisco Conference, a Gallup poll found that fifty-four per cent of our citizens believed America would have to fight another war within fifty years. In another Gallup poll on July 25, 1945, only fifteen per cent thought the United Unions would prevent war; twenty-seven thought it would *if* the nations continued to cooperate; thirty-six per cent thought it would not; and twenty-two per cent were undecided. The strong public sentiment for the adoption of universal military conscription, which continued after the Senate approval of the Charter, also indicated that most Americans were not pinning all their hopes on the new international agency.

While the majority of our citizens had substantial reservations about the peace-keeping potential of the United Nations, there was an articulate minority who were considerably more optimistic in their appraisal. Many leaders of religious and other service-oriented organizations were active members of this minority.

Some of these people regarded the United Nations as mankind's best hope for peace, as a new gateway to a world of harmony and cooperation. Others who would also call themselves "internationalists" looked upon the United Nations primarily as a channel through which our nation could express more effectively than ever before its responsibilities to the world community. Some ardent supporters of the United Nations, perhaps motivated by unacknowledged isolationist sentiments, regarded the organization as an actual or potential substitute for traditional diplomacy, military alliances, balance-of-power strategies, national military forces, and eventually for "power politics" itself. Several students of the American character believe that a substantial number of the most vocal United Nations advocates were motivated in part by a subconscious desire to escape from the hard realities of world politics and the new responsibilities of the United States. They believed that, if the United Nations could keep the peace by crushing any would-be aggressor, this heavy and distasteful responsibility would not fall upon our country as it did in two World Wars; therefore, they supported the United Nations. Psychologically, politically, and perhaps morally, the line between an idealistic internationalist and a political isolationist is often very thin. Both positions tend to lead toward the abdication of national responsibility in international affairs.

Twelve years have passed since the United Nations came into being. The peace has not been kept. There was a bloody war in Korea with more than two million casualties. The majority judgments of the United Nations have been flouted frequently by the Soviet bloc and occasionally by Britain, France, Egypt, Israel, and India. Conflicting national interests persist. The world is tragically torn by a Cold War, although it has entered a new and perhaps less belligerent phase. Both camps in the Cold War have erected military alliances outside the structure of the United Nations. Today the United States still finds it necessary to maintain almost three million men in uniform, over a million of whom are stationed in sixty-three foreign lands. The nuclear arms race continues unabated.

The history of the last twelve years has not ratified the high expectations of those who thought of the United Nations as a substitute for "power politics." It has confirmed the more sober assessment of the United Nations held by the majority of Americans. The position of those who still regard the United Nations as an actual or potential alternative to the tragedies and contingencies of world politics appears to be rooted in a Wilsonian world view. Some of these present-day Wilsonians believe that the League of Nations failed because the United States was not a member. Today the situation is vitally changed. Our Government is not only a charter member of the United Nations, but it was the most active government calling for its establishment. The United States is now committed to the world organization and is determined that it shall succeed. This confidence in the United Nations is also rooted in the belief that the methods of representative democracy, which worked so well in America's domestic experience, could be applied directly to the realm of international politics. The United Nations, unlike the League, presents a parliament-like setting for the practice of the principles of democracy in international diplomacy. These legalistic assumptions about the efficacy of international charters and "peace machinery" are usually based upon an optimistic view of the rationality and moral capacity of men and nations and the belief that conflicts between nations are caused by superficial blemishes, such as simple ignorance and misunderstandings which can be dealt with by education and by legal and judicial devices.

Some of the latter-day Wilsonians have become disillusioned with the United Nations because it has failed to meet their great expectations. Others still believe the United Nations would match their earlier hopes "if only the nations would give it their full support." These idealists constantly admonish our Government not to "bypass the U.N." Perhaps the majority of those who expected too much in 1945 now explain the yawning gulf between their hopes of yesterday and the tragic realities of today by admitting that their hopes were wrong. Their high expectations have been chastened by the realities of the past twelve years. They have not given up hope for a more peaceful and secure world. They believe that our Government can pursue a sound and responsible foreign policy which will contribute to international peace and security. They view the United Nations with a new sense of realism, recognizing it as both a living symbol of our hopes for peace and an actual instrument which can be used, abused, or ignored by its member states. They recognize that the United Nations is a child of Wilsonian idealism and a temporary wartime coalition and accept the fact that its character must reflect both parental strains.

A Conference of Sovereign States

There are two United Nations organizations, the one described in the San Francisco Charter and the one which has actually operated in a world divided by a Cold War and torn by political, economic, and racial struggle in Asia and Africa. In this chapter we will be concerned mainly with the political United Nations as it has actually operated, and not with the legal United Nations of the Charter, in so far as the two can be separated.

The United Nations is fundamentally a continuing conference of eighty-one sovereign states pledged to uphold the high principles of its Charter. As an ideal the United Nations has a symbolic and moral power which transcends the member states, but as an organization it has no independent existence or power apart from the existence and power of its member governments. The latent moral force of the United Nations ideal becomes an active political force in world affairs only when its members as sovereign states pursue policies which contribute to international peace and security. The United Nations is not a repository of political power, but a channel through which the power of sovereign states may flow. Mrs. Franklin D. Roosevelt once said, "The United Nations is not a cure-all. It is only capable of effective action when its members have a will to make it work."

The United Nations is a voluntary association of nation-states, and not an international government. It can neither pass laws nor enforce them. The United Nations is not a "town meeting of the world" or a "parliament of man." Its constituents are sovereign governments, not individual citizens. Among these governments there does not exist sufficient moral or political consensus to support a common and enforceable international law on any of the really important political questions which divide the world. In March 1957 the United Nations General Assembly concluded its eleventh session without being able to define the word about which most of its debates centered—*aggression.* Ever since 1933, when the matter was first given to a League of Nations committee, the governments of the world have not been able to arrive at a common definition of aggression. They will probably never arrive at a satisfactory legal definition of aggression because it is not a legal question. It is rather a political and moral question which must be defined by the nations themselves in terms of their purposes and interests.

The United Nations has no independent political authority. The decisions arrived at by the majority of members of the Security Council or the General Assembly are not legally binding or politically enforceable. The United Nations can employ no sanctions to force compliance with majority judgments, although it can recommend that member nations employ sanctions against an erring member.

The existence of the United Nations, like the League of Nations before it, does not change the basic realities of world politics. The locus of political power and moral responsibility in international affairs remains where it has been for the past three hundred years—with the governments of sovereign nation-states. The United Nations cannot end the Cold War, slow down the arms race, or prevent World War III. The decisions of war and peace are made by the governments of nation-states, and at the present time especially by the governments of the two superpowers, the Soviet Union and the United States. The United Nations cannot transcend the conflicts of the Cold War. As a conference which includes the major antagonists as well as uncommitted powers it must reflect the bipolar struggle of our time. The United Nations is not a substitute for "power politics," military alliances, balance-of-power strategies, or traditional diplomacy, nor is it a panacea for the tragedies and vicissitudes of history. As a conference of sovereign states, it is essentially a supplementary instrument of foreign policy for its member governments.

The Limits of a Moral Symbol

For millions of people the United Nations has become a living symbol of international cooperation and world peace. It is a symbol of the world we want even as it reflects the world we have. The member nations have pledged to uphold the Charter which affirms "faith in fundamental human rights, in the dignity and worth of the human person, in equal rights of men and women and of nations large and small." Each member has pledged not to use armed force "save in the common interest" and "to employ international machinery for the promotion of the economic and social advancement of all peoples." These are high principles to which the nations are solemnly pledged, but it is difficult to ascertain whether the creation of the United Nations has actually contributed to an emerging consensus of values in the world. Values are more than phrases in a Charter—they are the effective loyalties which determine behavior. Who can say whether or not the international behavior of the United States, the Soviet Union, Great Britain, or India has improved since these nations signed the United Nations Charter?

Some ardent supporters of the United Nations tend to confuse its symbolic value with its political potential. A symbol of international peace may or may not contribute to the realization of the ideal it symbolizes. Peace and security are the result of many political, economic, psychological and moral forces. Even the moral ingredients of political decision—the wisdom to know the way to peace and the willingness to pay the price—springs from sources far more substantial than mere symbols of peace. Such moral qualities are rooted in the basic character and values of a people and reflect their entire religious and cultural heritage. Yet in every generation men need fresh and tangible symbols of their highest aspirations. For many persons today the United Nations is the symbol of their hope for peace.

Reinhold Niebuhr has warned religious leaders against the dangers of repeated affirmations of loyalty to the United Nations, pointing out that it is only the symbol and "most current vehicle" of international cooperation. It is easy, he said, to become committed to "international cooperation in the abstract" and forget "those daily acts of fidelity" which make international cooperation a reality.[3]

Although it is not possible to measure the effect of the general moral symbolism of the United Nations on the behavior of its members, it is possible to assess the effect of the "moral voice" of the United Nations as it is expressed in the majority votes of the General Assembly or Security Council. Some governments are obviously more responsive to the "moral conscience" of a majority vote than others. During the 1946-1949 conflict between the Netherlands and Indonesia the Dutch government on several occasions complied with the "moral judgment" of the United Nations. On the other hand, the majority vote in the General Assembly condemning racial discrimination in the Union of South Africa seemed to harden that nation's official racial policy. In the past several years both Egypt and Israel have failed to comply with United Nations resolutions, and in the 1956-1957 Suez crisis Britain, France, and Israel flouted majority decisions of the General Assembly. India has refused to comply with the moral judgment of the United Nations on the question of Kashmir. Does the compliance of the Dutch government and the noncompliance, at least for a period, of these other governments mean that the Dutch government is morally superior to the British or Indian governments? Or does it mean that nations will simply defy the moral judgment of the United Nations when it is in their interest to do so and when they have the power to back up their defiance? Are resolutions of the United Nations effective only with the weak? Or perhaps the noncomplying governments had doubts about the moral wisdom or authority of the United Nations majority votes in their particular cases. (This raises a basic question about the moral status of majority decisions at the United Nations which will be dealt with in the following section.)

The Soviet Union, of course, presents an entirely different problem from that of the occasional non-complying nation. The Soviets are less influenced by moral judgments of the United Nations than any of the other member states. The Soviet Union and its satellites have frequently flouted majority decisions, especially on basic security questions, including the Communist aggression in Korea in 1950 and the Soviet suppression of Hungary in 1956. The position of the Soviets is quite understandable. It reflects both the balance of power within the United Nations and the basic political philosophy which motivates the Soviet leaders. Until about 1955 the United States and her allies could elicit majority support on any major issue; therefore, the Soviet Union was forced to exercise her legal veto in the Security Council and her political veto in the world of real politics. She felt that the rest of the world was against her and that it was thus necessary to protect her interests.

The Soviet Union took this position because she re-garded herself as the "chosen nation" to bring redemp-tion to all mankind. Her leaders were high priests of a political religion based on the philosophy of Marx and Lenin. Consequently her policies, both national and international, were by definition morally right, if not always politically sound. It was, therefore, utterly impossible for Soviet leaders to accept the validity of judgments resulting from the parliament-like debate at the United Nations, especially since the debate included "capitalist" and other governments "beyond the pale." Even within its own borders the Soviet ruling elite does not wish to have political questions seriously debated. The Communist world is a closed society in which the ruling class imposes its predigested "answers" upon the people. In July 1956, after the Kremlin had denounced the "excesses" of Stalin and before the October revolution in Poland and Hungary, *Pravda* found it necessary to emphasize the role of the Communist party as "the only master of the minds and thoughts of the people." At the same time the Soviet Central Committee issued a strong resolution against criticism of the present leaders and the basic Communist system.

Consequently, the eight hundred million subjects of the Soviet-Chinese empire are not exposed to the corrective and restraining influence of "world public opinion" or "the moral conscience of mankind" as it is expressed in the United Nations, since their government-controlled press gives them, with rare exceptions, only its own official version of the problems and issues of international politics. Even if sectors of the Soviet public were to succeed in getting a fairly accurate picture of what was happening at the United Nations through unjammed Voice of America or British broadcasts, there would be no adequate political channels through which their modified opinions and preferences could effectively influence national policy. In countries which have a free press the "moral judgments" expressed at the United Nations are known to the public, and active pressure groups sometimes force their government to conform to these "judgments." Lester B. Pearson, as Canada's Secretary of External Affairs, observed that decisions of the United Nations "carry great weight with the more responsible governments of the world." In a sense, the moral pressure of the United Nations is most effective where it is least needed; that is, in countries where internal moral and political restraints on national policy operate most freely.

The Moral Validity of Majority Decisions

Many people seem to assume that in principle the majority is always "right." If the majority is always "right" (and *right* is always a relative term), certainly the majority decisions of the United Nations, arrived at after prolonged debate, are right. This assumption can be challenged at many points. Under ideal conditions it might be assumed that decisions which have been arrived at democratically are right most of the time, but conditions are rarely ideal. There is nothing inherently just or wise about a majority decision in any human group. Even after prolonged and careful debate the majority decision may be morally wrong and politically unwise, since all human decisions reflect the limited intelligence, understanding, knowledge, and interests of those who make them. Since all men are fallible, self-interested, and morally ambiguous, their decisions, whether in the minority or the majority, reflect their rational and moral frailties. Nevertheless, since one man's interest may cancel out another man's interest, one man's wisdom offset another man's stupidity, and one man's knowledge make up for another man's ignorance, a majority decision based upon adequate debate may often be wiser than and morally superior to a minority decision.

All the human limitations which prevent some decisions from being right or wise in the parliament of any well-ordered state are magnified in the General Assembly, which is now the central organ of the United Nations. There is no assurance that decisions of the General Assembly will be morally right or politically sound, because these decisions always reflect the interests of national governments which may be politically destructive and therefore morally indefensible. The combined interests of a number of states do not necessarily add up to the larger interest of international peace and security. The matter is further complicated by the fact that every country, large or small, votes on every question, whether that country has a vital and intimate or a remote and tangential interest in the matter. Disinterestedness may be a vice as well as a virtue. The vote of a disinterested or uninterested power may be uninformed or irresponsible precisely because that power has little or no stake in the decision. Is not a disinterested nation more likely to sell its vote on an issue it regards as tangential in order to buy support for its position on another issue which it regards as vital? Is it morally responsible for Chile or Ghana to cast the deciding ballot on an issue of vital interest only to France and Germany? Is it not true that nations, like individuals, have a moral responsibility commensurate with their power? And if the responsibility of nations in the world of politics is commensurate with their power, should not their authority and influence be commensurate with their responsibility? The desirable balance between power, influence, and responsibility is maintained in the real world of international politics, but at the United Nations it is upset because the small nations and the disinterested nations enjoy far more influence than their status warrants. The concessions to the realities of world politics and the demands of moral responsibility reflected in the structure of the Security Council with its big-power veto are not present in the General Assembly. Hence the majority judgments of the Assembly may on certain occasions represent political unwisdom or moral irresponsibility.

Until recent years, the moral status of majority decisions at the United Nations was not a live issue in the free world, since the West always had the assurance of sufficient votes in the Assembly to uphold its policy on any important issue. But with the admission of many new members from Africa and Asia, the West can no longer depend on a working majority to support its position. "From this fundamental weakness," says Walter Lippmann, "come the confusions, the equivocations, the double standards of the United Nations' dealings with the Soviet Union over Hungary, with India over Kashmir, with Britain, France, and Israel over Suez and Gaza and the Gulf of Aquaba . . . in the General Assembly there is no effective majority which is willing to apply the same rule of law to the Soviet Union, India, Britain, France, Egypt, and Israel." [4]

An American policy of relying on and complying with the majority decisions of the United Nations is tenable only as long as the United States believes these decisions to be just and right from her point of view. With the present composition and voting patterns of the General Assembly, the time may not be far distant when the United States can no longer accept the moral validity of a majority vote. In the present Assembly of eighty-one member states, fifty-four votes, a two-thirds majority, are required to pass any important resolution. On any issue of great importance to the West the maximum number of votes which can be relied upon to support the position of

its leader, the United States, is forty-two. This includes the Americas, the British Commonwealth, and
our European allies. Forty-two votes are twelve votes
short of a working majority. Arrayed against the
United States and nations friendly to her are eleven
Soviet votes, eleven Arab votes, and sixteen votes of
the Afro-Asian bloc. On many issues four of the sixteen Afro-Asian nations—the Philippines, Nationalist
China, Thailand, and Pakistan—vote with the West.
Even with these four votes, eight more are needed
for a majority. These must be obtained by bargaining with "uncommitted" India. "This means," says
Walter Lippmann, "that the United States, working loyally through the United Nations, can on the
crucial issues take no positive or affirmative position
to which Mr. [Krishna] Menon is seriously opposed.
We cannot stand up for what we think is right and
just unless we are willing, which we are not, to have
a showdown which proves to the world that we are
no longer a part of the effective and ruling majority
of the United Nations." [5]

To put it another way, neither the West nor the
East commands a two-thirds working majority, and
each can veto any positive measure of the other.
"This deadlock can be broken," says Lippmann, "only
if certain of the great powers—on the Western side
the United States, on the Eastern side the Soviet
Union or India—switch sides. This is what happened
in the Egyptian affair when the United States voted
on the same side as did the Soviet Union and India.
There was no stalemate and the United Nations took
effective action to compel the withdrawal of Britain,
France, and Israel from Egypt. But there has been no
corresponding switching of sides, as there needed to
be, to apply equal pressure to Egypt. There has, of
course, been no equal pressure about Hungary and
none about Kashmir. If Algeria were taken up by the

United Nations the whole pressure would be on France, and none on the Arab nationalists. The fact of the matter is that the veto is always applied one way and not always applied the other way. For that reason the General Assembly is proving itself to be incapable of carrying out the prime purpose of the United Nations, which is to promote the peaceful settlement of conflicts."[6]

In the present General Assembly the Afro-Asian bloc can and probably would veto any American proposal designed to increase the military and political position of the Western coalition. Under these circumstances it would be foolhardy for the West to bring before the United Nations any matter on which it would risk defeat. For those who believe that the West has in the main pursued policies consistent with the larger interests of international peace and security, the present prospects in the United Nations are not bright.

A Vehicle of International Cooperation

Although the existence of the United Nations does not alter the basic realities of world politics, the organization does provide one additional channel through which nations can pursue their common interests and accommodate their conflicting interests so that international peace and security may be enhanced. Prior to the establishment of the United Nations, all the essential functions of diplomacy were carried out through traditional channels which, in addition to embassies and legations, included occasional international conferences and a number of permanent international agencies designed to deal with certain technical problems. The basic assumption underlying the idea of the United Nations is that some of these functions, especially those involving the interests of many states, can be performed more effectively through an inclusive and permanent international agency than through traditional channels. The United Nations with its eighty-one member states provides a continuing and almost universal instrument of cooperation among sovereign powers. The existence of the United Nations, of course, is no guarantee that it will be used by its members to advance the high purposes of the Charter to which they are pledged.

In behalf of its member governments the United Nations coordinates certain political and nonpolitical foreign policy functions. Among the nonpolitical functions performed through the United Nations are technical services such as international post, telecommunication, aviation, and meteorology. The most publicized nonpolitical services are concerned with the raising of living standards in the less-developed areas of the world. The humanitarian work of the World Health Organization, the Children's Fund, and the Technical Assistance Program is well known and widely supported by many religious and other service-oriented groups in the United States. Also important, though less dramatic, are the services performed by the World Bank and the International Monetary Fund. All these activities have had the support of the United States Government. These nonpolitical activities supplement bilateral governmental programs, private business enterprise and philanthropic work. The combined contribution of all such efforts helps to build the economic base for sound political and cultural development.

International economic and humanitarian programs may or may not make a contribution to international peace. Such efforts sometimes feed unrest and stimulate conflict. American economic aid to China probably helped the Communists to take over the Chinese government. Humanitarian activities and technical assistance merit support because they help the peoples of less-developed areas to a better life, and not because they offer a fool-proof guarantee of greater peace and security now or in the future. Any government, of course, has the right and duty to withhold its support from the social and economic programs of the United Nations, if it believes that such efforts jeopardize its own security or international peace. The Soviet Union has refused to participate in many of these programs. Most countries in the West, however, believe that technical assistance from the United Nations, for example, not only contributes to better living standards but also to the long-range objective of international security. There is a danger in supporting the nonpolitical functions of the United Nations only if too much is expected of them or if they are thought of as a substitute for the hard task of coming to grips with the profound political differences which divide nations. Exterminating grasshoppers and feeding undernourished babies are laudable activities in their own right, but they are never a substitute for the more immediate political tasks of defending national security or keeping the peace. Preoccupation with these humanitarian services may distract us from the primary political task for which the United Nations was established.

Greater intercultural understanding and respect for basic human rights are promoted by members of the United Nations through agencies such as UNESCO and the commissions on Human Rights and the Status of Women. The effectiveness of these efforts in a given country depends upon the degree of freedom which the United Nations has to operate in the country, the nature of the moral and political climate there, and other factors over which the United Nations agency has little control. The belief that intercultural understanding necessarily makes a contribution to international peace is based on the illusion that the conflicts which divide nations are due primarily to misunderstanding and ignorance. The Judaeo-Christian tradition holds that all human conflict is rooted in the sinful nature of man. Programs of education, pleas for goodwill, bills of human rights or legal structures will not remove these basic conflicts of interest, although these devices may help to mitigate and redirect conflicts.[7]

The U.N. and the Western Coalition

The primary purpose of the United Nations is to coordinate the policies of its member governments in the interests of greater international peace and security. This is essentially a political responsibility. The United Nations has been far more successful in its nonpolitical task than in its political task. As a voluntary conference of sovereign powers the United Nations cannot transcend but must reflect the Cold War struggle. Consequently, all significant security policies of the Soviet bloc and the Western coalition have been undertaken outside the structure of the United Nations. The existence of two competing security systems is both a cause and symptom of the impotence of the United Nations as an instrument for dealing with Cold War issues. Since the United Nations is incapable of dealing with major issues of international security, the government of the United States does not regard our participation in both the United Nations and the Western alliance system as morally or politically incompatible.

The fact that both sides in the bipolar struggle have sought to protect their security in arrangements outside the United Nations, does not mean that the United Nations has had no influence on Cold War issues. The contrary is true, for, as Reinhold Niebuhr observed in 1952, "The United Nations is a minimal bridge between the Communist and free worlds and an organ for integrating the free world." The over-all political effect of the United Nations for the first decade of its existence was to serve as a moral sanction for the Western coalition on all major issues. Majority votes both in the Security Council and the General Assembly have frequently supported security efforts of the free-world coalition. The most dramatic example was the Korean War. The majority of nations have sided with the United States, not because we coerced them with our superior power but because they believed that our policies were more consistent with their own national interests and with the larger interests of international security than were the policies of the Soviet bloc. This is a tribute to the quality of America's purpose as well as a recognition of the realities of power in our tragically divided world.

In minor conflicts which did not involve the vital security interests of either side in the Cold War, the United Nations has performed a useful service. In Greece, "watchdog" commissions of the United Nations helped to focus the attention of the free world on Soviet satellite aid to Communist guerrillas. This "moral pressure" helped to end the fighting there, although it was the Truman Doctrine that actually saved Greece as an independent state. In the clash between India and Pakistan over the disputed state of Kashmir, a United Nations commission helped to negotiate a cease-fire agreement, but as yet the United

Nations has not been able to force Mr. Nehru to comply with its resolutions ordering a plebiscite in Kashmir. The United Nations negotiated an uneasy armistice between Israel and the Arab states in 1949, and in the 1956-1957 Middle Eastern crisis it succeeded in persuading the British, French, and Israelis to withdraw their troops from Egypt; however, at this writing the United Nations has not "solved" any of the basic problems which underlie the unrest in this area. The fighting between the Dutch and Indonesian troops was twice stopped with the aid of the United Nations.

In these instances where hostilities were stopped, reduced or prevented, the facilities provided by the United Nations seem to have played a useful role. But the basic preconditions for the settlement of any dispute always lie deeper than the mechanism through which negotiation or mediation takes place, even if the mechanism is identified with a universal moral symbol. The indispensable ingredient in any agreement is the willingness of each party in the dispute to make the necessary concessions for the resolution of the conflict. This willingness is the product of many factors: the relative power position of the two sides; the views of allies; domestic political and moral pressure; and the "opinions of mankind" as expressed in majority judgments at the United Nations, especially as these judgments are transmitted through domestic channels. The good offices of the United Nations mediator may help to persuade a reluctant government to relax its demands, but his services are not a substitute for the more basic political and moral factors which bear upon the problem. Agencies of mediation and negotiation in labor-management disputes or in disputes between governments are useful only when the conflicting parties have the will to compromise their differences. Third-party agencies cannot provide this will and are useless without it. The United Nations, of course, is something more than a neutral third party, since it represents certain principles of international conduct to which the disputing parties have subscribed. But even so, the mere presence of a common moral symbol cannot force a government to redefine radically its understanding of its national interest. Vague moral principles are among the least effective factors in political decision.

If one believes that the major policies pursued by the United States and her allies during the first postwar decade were in general consistent with the goals of international peace and security, one can conclude that the United Nations has served well not only the interests of the United States and the Western coalition, but the larger interests of the international community for which it was established. The United Nations has supported and helped to modify the goals and strategy of the Western coalition in four ways:

First, the majority votes at the United Nations have provided a moral sanction for the policies of the free-world coalition. When the United States decided to repel the attack on South Korea, the majority endorsement went beyond moral support. Britain, France, Greece and other governments sent troops. India sent medical aides. Most United Nations members assisted in some tangible way under the banner of the United Nations Command. This united action was possible only because of the prior decision of the government of the United States and because the United Nations was directly involved in the Korean problem before the 1950 attack.

Second, participation in the United Nations, as in all forms of genuine international cooperation, imposes upon member governments certain moral and political restraints. This discipline of partnership can be of special value to superpowers which, because of their great power, lack of diplomatic experience, or a misguided sense of destiny, might be tempted to act unwisely and irresponsibly. The North Atlantic Treaty, which imposes a far heavier and more specific commitment on its members than does the United Nations, has probably had a more effective moral restraint on national action than the United Nations. But one should not underestimate the restraining effect of United Nations decisions on the behavior of free and responsive governments. Many Americans, for example, are sensitive to criticism of United States foreign policy voiced at the United Nations, especially if it comes from a respected ally or neutral power. On occasion they will urge the modification of a policy or proposed policy of our government to conform to what they regard as the valid "moral judgment" of a United Nations majority vote. Further, the constant exposure of our diplomats and the American people generally to the publicly-expressed viewpoints of other governments, especially when they are critical of our policies, makes some impact on the over-all behavior of our government. This impact may not always be in the right direction, but in general it would seem safe to assume that the criticism of allies and even unfriendly powers is a wholesome and necessary influence.

Criticism of United States foreign policy is not restricted to speeches and votes in the United Nations. It is always being expressed publicly by statesmen and journalists throughout the world and privately in diplomatic conversations. The open meetings at the United Nations serve to publicize views already well known to our officials. In general this is probably beneficial, although it has its limitations. Sometimes individuals or pressure groups, which take into account only the most publicized aspects of a complex international issue, place irrational and irresponsible demands upon our policy makers. The wide public knowledge today of the views of other governments on the policies of our own government makes it imperative that both citizen and statesman develop critical faculties for judging the relative merit of conflicting appraisals. It is not enough to assume, for example, that the Indian view or the British view of the United States is always right or always wrong.

Third, in the darkest days of the Cold War, when traditional diplomatic activity was at its lowest ebb, the United Nations served as a "minimal bridge" between the Communist bloc and the free world. When the United Nations is in session it offers the United States quick access to allies, neutrals, and hostile governments and provides atmosphere conducive to private, informal, and almost casual conversation. In making possible these "off-the-record" contacts, the United Nations made its greatest supplementary contribution to traditional diplomacy. Conversations between the Soviet Union and the United States leading to the lifting of the Berlin blockade were said to have taken place in the corridors of the United Nations headquarters. However, the diplomatic value of public sessions of the Security Council and the General Assembly has been widely questioned.[8]

Fourth, through United Nations agencies the Western coalition has been able to make a contribution to higher living standards and economic development in a number of uncommitted nations. This aid has helped to provide the economic base for domestic political stability and under certain conditions it has tended to make the peoples in these areas less susceptible to Communist propaganda and subversion. The multilateral programs of technical assistance and economic aid and the humanitarian services carried on through the United Nations have been worthy supplements to bilateral and multilateral programs such as the American Point-Four program and the British-sponsored Colombo Plan.

Future United Nations Policy of the United States

It appears clear that the United Nations, at least until 1955, served a useful instrument of the Western coalition. The changed composition of the United Nations brought about by the acceptance of sixteen new member states, in 1955, and the practice of bloc voting have produced the present situation, in which neither side in the Cold War can command the required two-thirds majority to put through any proposal of vital importance. Each side has a veto power over any affirmative action by the other. This deadlock can be broken only under extraordinary circumstances, when a major power of one side shifts its vote to the other. Faced with this dilemma, what should United States policy toward the United Nations be? Three major alternatives present themselves: 1) the United States could place full reliance on the majority decisions of the United Nations, complying with any decision affecting her interests; 2) she could place limited reliance on the United Nations, or 3) she could withdraw from the United Nations entirely.

The situation in the United Nations would have to deteriorate much further than it has before the United States would seriously consider withdrawing. The wide public support for the United Nations idea would make it virtually impossible for our government to abandon the organization unless it could convince the supporters of the United Nations that continued participation was in fact a barrier to a responsible foreign policy. So, as long as the United States receives even limited benefits from membership she will probably remain a member. If either the United States or the Soviet Union decides that the United Nations is no longer worth the effort, the United Nations will cease to exist and go the way of the League of Nations. The real alternatives open to the United States have to do with the extent of her reliance on the United Nations.

During the first months of the 1956-1957 Middle Eastern crisis, the pronouncements and policies of the Eisenhower Administration gave many observers here and abroad the impression that it was placing full reliance on the majority decisions of the United Nations. In Britain some political leaders feared that the President would do nothing to oppose the Soviet Union or to stabilize peace in the Middle East unless he got a two-thirds vote authorizing him to do so from the General Assembly. As late as his February 20, 1957 speech, President Eisenhower was urging Israel to place "its trust in the resolutions of the United Nations," with the clear implication that the United States was doing precisely this. This real or apparent over-reliance on the United Nations was widely interpreted as a disastrous abdication of American responsibility. Since the United States was the only Western nation with sufficient power to act decisively in the Middle East, the responsibility for leadership fell squarely upon her. She could not evade her heavy responsibility by turning the matter over to the United Nations. The policy of letting the United Nations make our policy for us is based on the wholly erroneous assumption that the United Nations is a supranational entity which, after careful deliberation, hands down just and impartial judgments. This assumption fails to take into account the fact that our government is a vital part of the United Nations and that the decisions made there are decisions in which we participate either by active leadership or by default. The assumption also fails to acknowledge that the decisions of the United Nations are not impartial but interested decisions, reflecting the interests of the nations which make them. To say, then, that the Middle Eastern policy of the United States is to refer the crucial matters to the United Nations is to answer only a procedural question. The real question has to do with the substance of United States policy, whether that policy is pursued unilaterally, in concert with selected allies, or through the United Nations.

It is difficult to believe that the Eisenhower Administration really wanted and expected the United Nations to make our Middle Eastern policy for us. But it is also difficult to escape the conclusion that the policy of reliance on the United Nations was an admission that we did not have a viable policy of our own. If we did have such a policy, and if we believed in working through the United Nations, we should have taken our position in the United Nations and worked for its acceptance with all the vigor at our command. Perhaps a more valid and charitable explanation of the Administration's temporary over-reliance on the United Nations was that this was simply a tactic for gaining time so that the United States could go about the difficult task of policy-making through the normal processes of confidential negotiation.

At any rate, the announcement of the Eisenhower Doctrine for the Middle East in January 1957 made it clear that the United States was by no means putting all her diplomatic eggs in the United Nations basket. Actually the Administration seemed to be returning to the policy of limited reliance on the United Nations which our government has followed ever since 1947. This policy recognizes that the United Nations has from its inception been a limited instrument of national policy, and that since 1955 it has become even more limited as far as nations in the Western coalition are concerned. According to this view our government should utilize the instrumentality of the United Nations only in those situations in which the United Nations is capable of taking morally-just and politically-wise positions. And the United States will have to be the judge of what is just and wise. This policy will sound "nationalistic" or self-righteous only to those who do not understand that governments are morally bound to pursue the national purpose and the interests which flow from this purpose, or to those who regard the general direction of United States foreign policy as unworthy of moral support. Morally, we want policies which contribute to peace and justice, regardless of whether these policies are evolved by one nation, by ten nations, or receive the majority vote of the United Nations. It is the substance of policy that is important, and not the procedure or mechanism through which it was evolved or carried out. There are morally-good unilateral foreign policies and morally unjustifiable multilateral policies. A two-thirds majority vote of the General Assembly does not change a foolish and irresponsible resolution into a wise and responsible one.

Charter Revision and the Limits of Law

The British have taken the lead in suggesting a weighted voting system in the United Nations to bring the resolutions passed in the world organization more into harmony with the realities of world politics. Recognizing the present stalemate in which the Afro-Asian bloc can veto any affirmative proposal of the West, some British students of the problem suggest that the weight of the vote of a member state be determined by the size and power of that state. This change is desirable, the argument runs, because the Afro-Asian bloc has failed to use its great voting strength with a genuine sense of international responsibility. Secretary Dulles has associated himself with the principle of weighted voting, although he has endorsed no concrete proposals. As long as nations route some of their foreign policies through international parliament-like agencies and as long as their people continue to regard the majority decisions of such agencies as having some moral validity, there is probably some merit to proposals designed to make the United Nations reflect as accurately as possible the real constellation of power, purposes, and interests in world politics.

Proposals to make the United Nations more "realistic" should be sharply distinguished from "idealistic" efforts designed to "strengthen" the United Nations by giving it greater "authority." The "realists" would have the power distribution of the actual world reflected in the structure and practice of the United Nations. The "idealists," or at least some of them, want national sovereignty, or substantial portions of it, transferred to a world authority. One set of proposals insists on an accurate reflection of our present multi-state system of independent national sovereignties. The other set of proposals insists that the multi-state system be radically altered in the direction of world government. World Federalists, world government advocates, and others who believe the United Nations can be transformed into a supranational authority by revising its Charter and changing its structure fail to comprehend the limits of law and legal structures, especially in the international sphere.

Law, charters, and legally-oriented organizations, to be politically effective, must embody the moral and political consensus of the community to which they apply. Today there is no adequate consensus among the nations of the world to support an effective and enforceable body of law covering major political and security questions. If the nations cannot agree on a definition of aggression, how could they possibly agree on the proper distribution of power and authority in a supranational political structure? There is, of course, a substantial body of "international law" covering technical questions, such as the immunities of diplomats, which is quietly observed by most of the nations most of the time because it is in their mutual interest to do so. But fundamental law is quite a different matter. If the preconditions of effective law are not present, law is powerless. If the preconditions of effective law are present, law is inevitable. Any effort to strengthen the United Nations by revising its Charter will be meaningless and ineffective unless such actions reflect basic changes in the international political situation, in which case the constitutional changes would probably not be necessary. Law and legal structures are largely reflections of political and moral consensus; they are not the cause of this consensus.[9]

The United Nations has not changed the basic facts of world politics, nor has it shifted the locus of moral responsibility in international affairs. The fateful decisions of war and peace still fall squarely upon the governments of nation-states, and particularly upon the governments of the Soviet Union and the United States. There is no honorable way by which our government, or we the people of the United States, can escape this heavy burden.

CHAPTER FIVE

*For our own economic growth we must have continu-
ously expanding world markets; for our security we
require that our allies become economically strong.*

DWIGHT D. EISENHOWER, 1954

FOREIGN TRADE, AID AND INVESTMENT

Several months after Hitler invaded Poland on September 1, 1939, the German Information Office in
New York City distributed throughout the United
States a leaflet designed to justify Hitler's expansionist policy. The leaflet pictured two contrasting maps,
one of "little" Germany and the other of the combined world empires of Britain and France. Under
the map of Germany were these words: "The Aggressor!"

This bit of propaganda was tailored to fit a widely-
accepted theory of "the basic cause of war." This
theory, fashionable in the 1930's, held that wars were
caused by the existence of "have" and "have-not"
nations. A "have" nation is large and wealthy and is
very likely to be a colonial power. A "have-not" nation is small, poor, and without overseas territories.
The "have-nots," according to the theory, want and
deserve more of what the "haves" have. Hitler's propaganda experts were aware that this theory of
international conflict was popular in the United States
and they exploited it to the hilt. Germany was

presented as simply a "have-not" nation attempting to get her just share of real estate or *Lebensraum.*

The have-have-not theory enjoys little acceptance today. It was never an adequate explanation of war, much less a moral justification for it. Modern wars have been caused not by *have-not* states like Finland, Greece, or Thailand, but by *have* nations like Germany and Japan who want to become *super-have* nations. The have-not theory is but one variation on a persistent theme which holds that the determining factors in international politics are economic. This theme merits careful consideration.

Economic Forces and World Politics

There are other variations, old and new, on the theme that economic factors are the determining forces in international affairs, most of which appear to bear some relation to Karl Marx' theory of "economic determination." Statements like these are familiar: Get rid of poverty and you get rid of war . . . Peace and plenty go hand in hand. . . . Free trade is the road to peace . . . Capitalism is the basic cause of war because capitalist countries are bound to clash with one another in their competition for expanding markets . . . Modern technical nations go to war to prevent mass unemployment . . . War is caused by profit-hungry munition makers . . . A global TVA will bring peace and bread . . . Economic aid and technical assistance to underdeveloped areas are more important than military defense . . . And so on.

These economic interpretations of world politics ignore the fundamental fact that the causes of war and the conditions of peace are multiple and complex. Every international development and every foreign policy is the result of a multitude of political, military, psychological, and ideological factors as well as economic forces. International conflict and violence are rooted in the morally-ambiguous nature of man and are not imposed upon man by outside forces. The immediate cause of great wars in our century has been the existence of a government, or governments, powerful enough to wage war and willing to do so in the pursuit of certain political objectives. No economic changes within nations or between them, however far-reaching, will of themselves prevent the rise of ambitious and aggressive men to positions of national power in which they can threaten and initiate war.

This is not to suggest that there is no connection between economic factors and foreign policy. Economic factors impinge upon world politics in a thousand ways, and in some cases they may be the decisive factors, but they are not the *exclusive* or even the *primary* factors in international affairs. The fundamental decisions of war and peace are political decisions, and political decisions always reflect the values, ambitions, and interests of the men who make them. These decisions are not made by men acting alone, but by men working through and endowed with the power of national governments. The relation of international trade or technical assistance to peace and security can be understood only within the dynamic realm of world politics.

What Is Foreign Economic Policy?

In pursuing her national interests the government of the United States employs the various instruments of foreign policy. We have already discussed diplomatic and military instruments. In this chapter we are concerned with economic instruments. Our government's efforts to influence the economies of other countries and to modify the international economic situation constitute our foreign economic policy. Economic policies, like military policies, are designed to serve our over-all foreign policy objectives.

In this Cold War period our foreign economic policies must be judged in terms of their contribution to our ultimate goal of a secure and peaceful world in which government by consent can flourish, and our immediate objectives of discouraging further Communist aggression, of avoiding a total nuclear war, and of maintaining sufficient economic strength to compete successfully with the Communist bloc. To serve these objectives the United States needs free-world allies who are militarily, politically, and economically strong as well as morally committed to our common cause. Consequently, she has an interest in stable and productive economies throughout the free world. The United States has an interest in raising the living standards and morale of the peoples in the less-developed areas of Asia and Africa, in order that they may become strong independent states and thus better withstand Communist attack or subversion. However, there is no guarantee that economic aid or technical assistance will not under certain circumstances have the opposite effect.

Should Foreign Policy Be Humanitarian?

Men who recognize the fundamental rights of peoples everywhere are deeply concerned with efforts to erase poverty, illiteracy, and disease. Freedom from want is a desirable goal in its own right, even if efforts in that direction do not make an immediate contribution to United States foreign policy objectives or to world peace. A decent living standard and a productive economy can provide the material foundation for the community of justice and mutual helpfulness which God wills for all men. Many voluntary organizations carry on humanitarian programs in this country and abroad. Every responsible national government is concerned about the welfare of its people.

The question then arises: Should the government of one nation have a humanitarian concern for the people under the jurisdiction of other national governments? Most Americans agree that under certain circumstances the United States Government should supplement the humanitarian services of private American organizations to meet famine and other disasters abroad. Our government and private organizations have often joined hands in providing flood, famine, and earthquake relief to needy areas in various parts of the world. Little question has been raised as to the appropriateness of such action.

But a more difficult question arises: Should the foreign policy of a nation attempt to serve humanitarian objectives abroad? (We are using the word *humanitarian* in its usual sense to mean certain direct welfare services to persons as distinct from political action in the interests of collective objectives such as peace and security.) The answer is both yes and no. The primary aim of foreign policy is to serve the national purpose and the interests which flow from this purpose. In pursuing these national interests, which are largely political in character, humanitarian concerns may also be served, but this is incidental. Even the wealthy United States does not have the resources to give assistance to all who need it. Our government must choose carefully where and under what conditions it should give aid to a foreign government, and it must make these choices in terms of its basic foreign policy objectives. This is morally justifiable in so far as the objectives themselves are morally justifiable.

During the past decade and continuing into the present there has been a happy concurrence between the security objectives of the United States and certain supranational humanitarian values in Europe, Asia, and Latin America. Our government has been able to serve simultaneously national and more inclusive goals, both of which are legitimate and neither of which necessarily has a moral priority over the other. Policies like the Marshall Plan and the Mutual Security Program, which have been motivated largely by security considerations, have served both security and humanitarian objectives. On the other hand, policies like Point Four and the sending of grain to India, which may be said to be motivated in part by humanitarian considerations, have served both humanitarian and security objectives. It is impossible for a superpower like the United States to carry out any foreign policy which does not have security and defense implications. It is likewise almost impossible for any of our "security" policies to be completely devoid of humanitarian values.

This does not mean that American technical assistance to India, for example, should have military strings attached. This is probably unwise, even from the point of view of security. Our government wants India to be a strong and independent country which values its freedom. In a vital conflict between Communism and Western democracy, we believe a strong and independent India would stand with the West. Consequently, technical assistance with no strings attached probably makes a firmer contribution to our security objectives than aid which attempts to force India to declare for us prematurely and against her will. A free and friendly country is a greater asset than a reluctant and coerced ally. Many observers believe that in its first few years the Eisenhower Administration was more interested in concluding defense alliances in Asia than in helping to create the essential economic and political preconditions for free and responsible governments, but there are signs that this approach has been changing.

Amerian Prosperity and the World Economy

In order for the United States to pursue its over-all foreign policy goals effectively, there are certain foreign economic objectives which must be kept in mind. The five objectives listed here, which are calculated to serve us well during the Cold War and beyond, have wide acceptance both in the government and among the public: 1) to maintain a high level of income and employment in the United States, 2) to increase international trade and reduce or eliminate trade barriers, 3) to increase long-term American investment abroad, 4) to continue foreign economic aid and technical assistance to meet clearly established needs, and 5) to continue to cooperate with other nations in constructive programs for the promotion of world economic health. The relative success or failure in pursuing any or all of these economic objectives will have a significant impact upon the effectiveness of United States foreign policy as a whole.

Today there is probably nothing the Soviet Union

hopes for more fervently than the collapse of the American economy. Conversely, there are few things our allies fear more than an American depression or severe inflation. This Soviet hope and this allied fear spring from the same fundamental fact—the sheer weight of our unprecedented economic power has a tremendous effect on the entire world economy. We "export" both our depressions and the evil effects of our inflationary periods.

When we have a slight recession, we buy a far smaller volume of raw materials and manufactured goods from other countries. This decreases their badly needed dollar earnings, with the result that they buy less from us, thereby damaging their own economy and depressing our economy still further. When the opposite development, inflation, occurs in the United States, the prices of our raw materials and manufactured goods rise, forcing prices upward in the world market. This has an adverse effect on countries which need to import the items affected.

The ups and downs in the level of income and employment in the United States, with their inescapable impact on the volume and the prices of imports and exports, constitute the greatest single influence of the United States on the prosperity and economic stability of the rest of the world. The maintenance of a stable and high level of productivity in the United States is, therefore, the most important contribution to world economic stability and development our nation can make. Political stability and social development in other countries are dependent upon their domestic prosperity; all three suffer if the United States reduces her imports from abroad. In the present situation our high level of employment and expanding economic activity make an indispensable contribution to the strength of the free-world coalition.

Trade Is a Two-Way Street

The United States is a wealthy nation. With only six per cent of the world's population, she produces over forty per cent of the world's goods and services. Yet our country is dependent on imports from all over the world. If these imports were to be completely cut off, our daily life would change drastically until adequate substitute for vital imports could be found. Our automobiles, telephones, radios, television sets, and a hundred other modern necessities would become useless when parts depending on imports would wear out. We would be threatened with mass unemployment. And our defense program would collapse.

Every automobile needs thirty-eight essential materials which are largely imported. Forty-eight imported products go into every telephone. Not a single pound of steel can be made without manganese; nine tenths of our supply of this vital ore is imported. We import *all* of our chromium and tin, ninety-nine per cent of our nickel, sixty-five per cent of our bauxite (essential to making aluminum), forty-two per cent of our copper, and so on. On an average day about 418,000 tons of imports, worth forty-two million dollars, arrive at American ports. Only about one eighth of these imports are finished manufactured products which can compete with American-made goods. At the present time our annual imports total more than eleven billion dollars.

Other countries need our products and we need theirs. We need to export in order to buy the necessary imports for our own economic health. A substantial loss of foreign markets could damage our entire economy. The United States cannot export unless other countries have dollars to buy our products. To obtain dollars they must sell to us. Trade is a two-way street. If the traffic slows down on one side of the street, it will have to slow down on the other. A balanced and high-level flow of world trade makes for world-wide economic health. The interdependence of nations is nowhere more clearly apparent than in the economic realm.

Since the end of World War II political and economic conditions, including certain policies of the United States, have made it impossible for most countries to get the dollars they needed to buy the American goods they wanted. If Britain, for example, wanted to buy ten million dollars' worth of machine tools here and had only five million in dollar credits, she would be faced with a serious problem. She could decide to get along on half the tools needed. Or the United States, recognizing the value of strengthening an ally, could advance the needed five million in credits. This kind of situation occurred repeatedly in the first postwar decade, and billions of dollars' worth of credit was granted to war-shattered nations by the government of the United States, to enable them to buy from us.

Western Europe and Japan are now more productive than before the war, but they still are not so productive as the United States. Their inability to compete with American productivity in certain fields is aggravated by American trade and tariff restrictions. These restrictions are one of the major barriers to balanced trade with the United States, preventing the free world from utilizing at greatest efficiency its human and natural resources. If the United States accepted more imports, her domestic economy as well as the economy of the free world as a whole would benefit.

Some people wish to "protect" certain American industries from "damage" caused by competition from abroad. The important question is not the effect of imports on a certain industry, but their effect upon the economy as a whole. If a particular industry and its workers suffer undue hardship because of a more liberal tariff policy, the Government has a responsibility to help relocate those displaced into other productive enterprises. As Adlai Stevenson put it, "We shall have to make the choice between relatively minor adjustments caused by increased imports or major adjustments caused by decreased exports." President Eisenhower has said: "If we fail in our trade policy, we may fail in all. Our domestic employment, our standard of living, our security, and the solidarity of the free world—all are involved."

In December 1956, Mr. Eisenhower made a dramatic decision which demonstrated how our national trade policy is inextricably related to the security and economic welfare of both the United States and the free world. The President decided to reject a unanimous recommendation of the United States Tariff Commission to raise the duties on groundfish fillets which we import mainly from Canada, Norway, and Iceland. Our domestic fish industry had claimed that it was being "hurt" by these imports, and persuaded the Tariff Commission to recommend greater "protection." In his veto message the President said that it is our policy to "encourage in all feasible ways the continued expansion of beneficial trade among the free nations of the world" and refrain from imposing any unnecessary barriers to such trade, especially in a case of this kind in which the nations involved are "close friends" and in which the economic strength of the nation in question "is of strategic importance to us in the continuing struggle against the menace of world communism." Although the President said nothing about it in his message, it is generally understood that Iceland withdrew its long-standing request that American troops evacuate the NATO air base in Iceland with the understanding that Mr. Eisenhower would not permit the increased tariff on groundfish fillets. We import twenty-eight per cent of Iceland's groundfish exports.

Students of American trade policies have suggested eight ways for the United States to increase its imports: 1) The Reciprocal Trade Agreements program should be made permanent and the "escape" and "peril points" clauses eliminated. The Trade Agreements Act of 1934, as revised, authorizes the President to make agreements with other governments for the reduction of tariffs by as much as two thirds. By 1951 agreements under this act had been concluded with fifty-three different nations. Under the "escape" clause, added in 1951, an American producer may claim undue injury from imports and ask the Tariff Commission to recommend an increase in a duty previously reduced in a trade agreement. The "peril points" amendment, also added in 1951, requires the Tariff Commission to place limits on tariff reductions which cannot be exceeded by the President without an explanation to Congress.

To increase imports it is also recommended that 2) new legislation be enacted, permitting the United States to reduce tariffs without waiting for similar concessions from other countries, and that 3) further legislation be enacted to simplify import procedures. In addition to tariffs there are quotas, embargoes, processing taxes, and other restrictions, as well as a bewildering maze of complex customs regulations and procedures. These regulations should be consolidated and simplified to make it easier for exporters to sell their products here.

4) The repeal of "Buy American" legislation would also pave the way for increased imports. The "Buy American" act, passed in 1933 during the depression,

requires the federal government to buy domestic rather than foreign products unless this is "inconsistent with the public interest." In practice, American goods have often been purchased by the government even if they were more expensive than imports of equal quality. 5) There should be a careful study of our present regulations restricting agricultural imports with the view to finding a solution which would meet both our need for increased imports and the right of American farmers to economic security.

6) American citizens should be encouraged to travel and buy abroad. Tourist and educational travel is a major source of dollar income in many countries. In 1956 American tourists paid foreign countries more than one billion five hundred million dollars. 7) The present requirement that fifty per cent of United States foreign aid cargoes be carried on American-owned ships should be reconsidered in the light of the major purpose of our foreign aid program, which is to strengthen the economies of other nations. 8) The United States should join the Organization for Trade Cooperation, the international agency which administers the General Agreement on Tariffs and Trade to which we belong. In urging Congress to authorize American membership in the O.T.C., President Eisenhower in February 1957 said that this action would make our Trade Agreements Program more effective and contribute to international commerce which is "conducive to the establishment of a just and lasting peace in the world."

The United States is already a member of all United Nations economic bodies, such as the World Bank and the International Monetary Fund, as well as of many other international agencies devoted to furthering economic cooperation. The Bank and the Fund promote economic development and stability by making available low-interest loans to needy governments for approved projects. These international agencies help to strengthen both the economically developed and the less-developed countries of the free world, and thus contribute to our over-all foreign policy objectives.

*Foreign Aid, Technical Assistance, and
Investment*

In the first eleven years after World War II the United States spent approximately fifty-six billion dollars in foreign economic aid. During the five-year period between Hiroshima and the Korean invasion we appropriated twenty-six billion, of which one and one-half billion went for direct military assistance. The great bulk during these early postwar years, twenty-four and one-half billion, went to American-subsidized relief and rehabilitation programs in the war-torn countries of Europe and Asia. The Korean War reversed the picture. During the period of 1950 through 1956 we spent thirty billion in our assistant program, seventeen billion of which went for direct military aid. A very large portion of the remaining thirteen billion was spent for indirect military assistance. In the fiscal year 1956-1957, all but six hundred million of the three and seven-tenths billion dollars appropriated for foreign aid went for military purposes. During the entire eleven years of our aid program, only three and three-tenths billion was spent to assist underdeveloped countries.

Several things are clear from this brief summary of our economic aid program. We have stopped completely our relief and rehabilitation assistance, and now the great bulk of our money is spent to maintain our system of military alliances which was launched under President Truman and has been enlarged under Mr. Eisenhower. In the fiscal year 1955-1956, for example, nearly forty per cent of our appropriations was spent for military "hardware" and other military facilities for NATO. Another forty-five per cent went to subsidize the military efforts of allies such as Greece, Turkey, Iran, Pakistan, South Vietnam, Formosa, and South Korea. Military and economic aid to the Republic of Korea alone is now costing the United States about six hundred million dollars a year. We have spent a very small proportion, about six per cent, on Mr. Truman's "bold new program" of technical assistance to underdeveloped areas.

Most observers believe that our early foreign aid emphasis on relief and reconstruction made a tremendous contribution to the economic and political restoration of Japan and Western Europe, and as such was a sound American investment. The increasing emphasis on military aid after the Korean attack is also a sound investment, if one believes that our alliance strategy is itself a wise and defensible policy. Considering the gravity of the issues at stake in the Cold War and what the high cost of *not* giving aid might have been, it would appear that the economic and political accomplishments of the United States aid program, to say nothing of its modest humanitarian achievements, are ample evidence that the program has been eminently worthwhile.

In his inaugural address in 1949, President Truman called for a "bold new program for making the benefits of our scientific advances and industrial progress available for the improvement and growth of the underdeveloped areas." The proposal was *new,* but the response of the Congress could not be described as *bold.* Point Four assistance has been by far the least costly of our aid programs. The object of this program is to improve living standards by fighting man's ancient enemies of poverty, ignorance and disease. To accomplish this goal, specialists from the more-developed countries are sent to less-developed countries which request assistance. In addition to the American bilateral Point Four program, the United States contributes to the multilateral Technical Assistance Program of the United Nations. Such technical cooperation has often yielded significant results in raising the living standards in limited areas. But the need is vast and the surface has scarcely been scratched. The striking differences in economic development become clear when we compare various areas of the world. Setting the annual income of Asia at *one,* the income of Latin America is *three,* the income of Western Europe *eleven,* and the income of the United States *thirty-one.* The world average is *five.*

Some zealous advocates of the Point Four program have made extravagant claims in behalf of technical assistance. It should be remembered that technical aid to underdeveloped areas, however much it is needed, is only one aspect of United States foreign policy. It is not and cannot become a substitute for diplomacy, military defense programs, NATO, our foreign information program, or for other aspects of our foreign economic policy. Even the more strictly economic and humanitarian values of the program are seriously limited by factors over which we have little control. Raising the level of technology in India, for example, will have a limited effect on the over-all living standard there unless it is accompanied by land reform, birth control measures, increased trade, and substantial capital investment from abroad. The economic benefit from technical assistance is also enhanced by political factors such as effective local government, domestic stability, and national security.

Responsible support of Point Four must be based on a clear recognition of its limitations and possibilities. It is not a magic key to a new world of peace and plenty, and could not become so even if it were increased a hundredfold.

Point Four has already made a solid contribution, and with substantially increased resources it could become a great program for the relief of human misery which would also contribute to international peace and security. On its present modest scale it can help give people in dependent and recently dependent areas new hope for greater justice and freedom, and thus make Communist promises less appealing. It can help to lay the economic foundations for a healthy community. Many religious leaders, students of foreign policy, and other American citizens believe that our small commitment to this program is far from adequate and should be greatly increased. Speaking for many advocates of an expanded program of technical assistance, Reinhold Niebuhr says: "We need a re-examination of all American policies which have an impact on Asia and Africa, including our military posture, our Asian alliances, our position on colonialism and disarmament, our use of farm surpluses, and our administration of economic aid. . . . America, many Asians believe, has made military pacts, military threats, and predominantly military aid the heart of its policies toward Asia. And these are not the principle needs of Asia. The aspiration of the people is for rapid economic progress. The chief danger of communism, many Asian leaders are convinced, arises from a lack of economic and social progress, which frustrates the new educated classes, spurs political unrest, and gives subversion a greater prospect of success." [1]

In addition to her foreign aid program, the United States can help to stimulate the economic and technical development of less wealthy nations by investing capital abroad. The United States is the chief source of investment capital in the world today. The prospects for economic development in the poorer countries are severely limited due to the fact that their low national income does not make substantial saving and investment possible. Long-term private and governmental American investment should be increased because of its contribution both to the world economy and to the economy of the United States. Foreign investment often involves great risks, especially in countries where it is needed most. Governments seeking American capital should make investment in their economies as attractive and rewarding as possible.

The Future of United States Economic Aid

Ever since the outbreak of the Korean War there has been a growing reluctance on the part of Congress to support our economic aid program. In 1948 only eight Senators voted against the final passage of the Marshall Plan. In 1956 there were thirty Senate votes cast against the Mutual Security Appropriations bill. This increasing opposition in Congress to foreign aid reflects a confusion in the public mind about the aims, character, and accomplishments of our foreign aid program. This confusion is rooted in the fact that the program has multiple objectives, goals which in the minds of some persons run at crosspurposes with each other. It is difficult to understand a single program which seeks to raise standards of living in India, for example, and at the same time spend most of its money giving military aid to Chiang Kai-shek and Syngman Rhee. This confusion is further abetted by the fact that the Administration presents the program in different lights at different times in order to gain support at home or abroad. Foreign aid is sometimes presented primarily as a military program, which it actually is, and at other times the nonmilitary aspects are emphasized. If most nominal opponents really understood that our present program is overwhelmingly an effort to subsidize our far-flung military alliances, much of their opposition would disappear, unless they had serious misgivings about the validity of our alliance structure itself. Few members of Congress question programs which the Administration insists are vital to our national security.

The close connection of technical assistance to security considerations has been criticized by certain religious spokesmen who have urged that our aid program be "nonpolitical" and "humanitarian," and who suggest that the best way of accomplishing this objective is to channel our economic assistance through the United Nations. These critics fail to recognize that the governments of nation-states are not morally obligated to support "humanitarian" programs abroad in the name of humanitarianism. National governments must justify their foreign aid programs, or any other aspects of their foreign policy, in terms of their basic contribution to the national purpose and the interests which flow from it. An economic aid program conducted by the United States and designed to serve our national interests is not morally wrong unless the official definition of the national interest excludes a proper respect for the interests and rights of other nations. International politics and economics are inseparably intertwined. Political ethics is concerned with the quality of the politics and the total effect of the aid rather than with the fact that the two cannot be separated. A superpower can do nothing in the area of foreign economic policy without its action having significant political implications. Military power and economic power cannot be separated.

There are, however, sound political and strategic reasons why our military and our economic aid programs should be administered separately. This would avoid confusion in this country and abroad and would probably contribute to the greater effectiveness of both programs. It would also give Congress a clearer opportunity to judge each program on its own merits. Such a structural and administrative separation of the military and nonmilitary aspects of foreign economic aid does not mean that one program is more important than the other or that either program could be a substitute for the other. Nor does it mean that economic aid would cease to be a political instrument. Our ability to give or withhold aid cannot escape from being a weapon in the Cold War. We cannot wish this fact away. The moral problem has to do with the way the weapon is used and the purposes for which it is wielded. No one questioned the right of the United States to withdraw her offer to aid Egypt in building the High Dam at Aswan, but many persons have criticized the timing and the manner in which Mr. Dulles announced this withdrawal of aid.

During the spring of 1957, when Congressional support for foreign aid was at its lowest ebb since the program was launched, the reports and recommendations of three distinguished research agencies on the problem of economic aid were made public.[2] These three independent studies, prepared for the Senate Special Committee to Study the Foreign Aid Program, have helped to clarify the foreign aid picture. Each report called for the continuation of military aid and an enlarged program of technical assistance to the less-developed areas. The three reports made substantially the same recommendations: 1) that our foreign aid program should be planned on a long-term basis of perhaps twenty or thirty years; 2) that it should include an appropriation of approximately two billion dollars a year for technical assistance, which would be about eight times as much as we are now spending; 3) that it should be managed by the United States government, but in consultation with the aid programs of our Western allies and of the United Nations; 4) that it should be administered separately from the military assistance program, and that technical aid agreements should never be tied directly to mutual defense commitments; 5) that it should be supplemented by substantial capital investment from the United States; and 6) that it should make the fullest possible use of American farm surpluses consistent with responsible international trade practices.

About the same time that the three private reports were made public, the International Development Advisory Board, appointed by the President in 1950, issued its report on the problem of foreign aid.[3] The Board's recommendations were essentially the same as those of the independent reports. As a matter of fact, there was little new and startling about any of these reports; their proposals in most instances paralleled suggestions made by many religious leaders and other persons concerned with the problem since 1950.

What is to be said concerning the future of American economic aid? Certainly military assistance to our allies will continue as long as we have allies and alliances. The real question centers on the problem of technical cooperation. There is no lack of sound plans for long-terms assistance programs. What is lacking is the imagination to see the many values of such a program and the willingness to pay the relatively small price for it. It is the task of our statesmen and other concerned leaders to convince the American people that a well-conceived technical assistance and investment program is not only an indispensable ingredient in our over-all foreign policy in this era of competitive coexistence with the Soviet-Chinese empire, but that it would make a genuine contribution to the welfare of the peoples who receive our aid and serve the more inclusive goals of international peace and security.

CHAPTER SIX

What we are remains more important than what we say we are. Doing is more important than saying, or promising, or boasting.

GEORGE V. ALLEN, 1948

THE WAR OF WORDS AND IDEAS

In November 1955 Admiral Arthur W. Radford, Chairman of the Joint Chiefs of Staff, called upon the United States to launch a crusading "Free World ideology" which would be strong enough and dynamic enough to prevail over Communism in the global struggle for the minds of men. The strategy for this crusade was set forth in a pamphlet entitled *Militant Liberty,* issued by Admiral Radford's office and endorsed by Secretary of Defense Charles E. Wilson. A vigorous program to sell "Militant Liberty" is absolutely essential, said the pamphlet, because "the present Communist threat to the freedom of individuals and nations must be met by dynamic action. The Communists have made outstanding and amazing gains . . . because they know what they believe, why they believe it, and can explain it to people anywhere in understandable terms. . . . On the other hand, we, as a free people, who believe in the true form and ideals of liberty, have many times been incoherent and lacked the verbal ability to explain or defend completely what liberty is and thereby have forfeited the field to the Communists. The militant part of the concept concerns the spirit of the individual in positively proclaiming and explaining these truths of liberty." [1] The pamphlet adds, "Communist ideology can only be defeated by a stronger *dynamic* ideology. Therefore, the concept of Militant Liberty consists of explaining the ideas of liberty in a manner that will motivate peoples everywhere to exercise and collectively demonstrate the practices of a positive philosophy of Freedom."

At the time of its public launching, the "Militant Liberty" idea had been introduced into the courses of the National War College and the Air War College, and training kits were being prepared for the weekly world-wide troop education program, the curricula of the Military, Naval, and Air Academies, and college R.O.T.C. courses. In spite of its auspicious beginning, "Militant Liberty" was not enthusiastically received by the President, the State Department, Congress, or the American public. It has gone the way of other simple and grandiose schemes for dealing simultaneously with complex political and philosophical problems. This particular proposal for an "ideological offensive" is significant only because it embraced so many of the widespread illusions about the nature of foreign policy and political loyalty, and because an enterprising advocate was able to persuade the Chairman of the Joint Chiefs of Staff and the Secretary of Defense to endorse it. The author of the idea is John C. Broger, President of the Far East Broadcasting Company, a non-profit agency which beams programs into Asia from the Philippines and Formosa. Admiral Radford brought Broger to the Pentagon in 1953 to introduce the proposal. Mr. Broger's program is not original; in fact, it is typical of a number of proposals for "winning the war in the minds of men" which are based upon serious misconceptions about the nature and limitations of "propaganda warfare," "international persuasion," and foreign policy itself.

Persuasion and Foreign Policy

Ideas, values, and loyalties have always been essential ingredients in international politics and foreign policy. All governments must learn the art of persuasion at home and abroad or eventually they will perish. No government can exist without the consent of its people, although popular consent may be willingly or grudgingly given. No modern nation can pursue a foreign policy successfully without the willing or unwilling support of its citizens, who must be persuaded or manipulated into believing that the policies of their government are right or just or at least the best under the circumstances. This necessity to be concerned about what "the people" think is a product of the modern democratic creed which demands that the rulers take seriously the opinions and preferences of the citizens from whom they draw their power. Even totalitarian leaders have found it expedient to use the slogans and other external symbols of democracy as devices for wresting an unwilling consent from their people. This fact is a testimony to the strength of the democratic creed in the modern world and an unconscious recognition by these dictators of the very values they deny.

The government of any state must engage in international persuasion if it hopes to maintain or enhance its status, position and power in the incessant struggle of world politics. The necessity for a government at war to convince its enemies of its power and resolution and its allies of its sincerity and fidelity is widely acknowledged. Both generals and wartime diplomats draw heavily from the arsenal of "psychological warfare." The necessity of "psychological warfare" in time of peace is, however, not widely accepted. But if ideas, values, and loyalties are important in a shooting war, are they not even more important in an era of competitive coexistence such as the present one? Today, practically everyone would agree that "the struggle will ultimately be won in the minds of men," but this truism can mean almost anything from advocating a pacifist foreign policy to launching a full-blown ideological war.

The ever-present ideological factor in international politics has been intensified in our time by the rise of competing national political religions. Governments like those of Nazi Germany and the Soviet Union are motivated by political theologies which claim to provide *the* answer, not only to political and economic questions, but to the ultimate questions of human existence as well. The political imperialism of these governments is supported by an imperial ideology or political religion which is based in part on the nineteenth-century illusion that man can shape his destiny by calculation, planning and discipline. The dynamism of these national religions finds expression in all aspects of their foreign policies, and especially in their international propaganda programs. All the technical instruments of modern mass persuasion and manipulation are enlisted in the cause of promulgating their gospel at home and throughout the world. The ideological formulations of these crusading nations are in part a façade behind which the ruling elite conceals its naked drive for power, and in part a genuine attempt to express their contempt for the traditional values of Western culture by advancing alternative ultimate objectives. Political ideologies tend to demand not only the political loyalty of citizens but their spiritual allegiance as well. Their sweeping objectives and the loyalties they demand lead to total rather than limited wars.

The rise of political religions which challenge the traditional values of the Judaeo-Christian religion and the traditional concepts of limited government poses a profound problem for the Western democracies. In the face of this challenge, the United States must remain militarily and economically strong. She must pursue prudent policies in concert with her allies. But sound diplomatic, military, and economic policies are not enough in an era when the bookstalls and airwaves of the world are alive with ideas which challenge the validity of our basic political, economic, cultural, and religious institutions, and when the Soviet Union is poisoning the international atmosphere with gross distortions and falsehoods about the character, values, and foreign policy objectives of the United States. How shall we respond to this dual challenge? How shall the United States meet the ideological onslaught of the Soviet Union and World Communism? Shall she respond with a counter-ideology? In the face of the persistent and massive distortion of our image, how can we succeed in presenting a "full and fair picture" of ourselves?

The Soviet Image of the United States

In its world-wide effort to extol the virtues of Communism and to present a highly distorted picture of the character and objectives of the United States and its allies, the Soviet Union spends an estimated billion and a half dollars a year.[2] This campaign of falsehood began soon after the end of World War II and is carried on by radio, by the printed page, and by word of mouth throughout the world. Radio Moscow is broadcasting in many languages for a total of approximately three hundred hours per week, almost double the output of the Voice of America. The Soviet Union has a vast network for distributing millions of new and inexpensive books each year. According to a UNESCO survey of the "world's most translated authors" from 1948 to 1955, Lenin led the list with 968 different translations.[3] Second came the Bible with 887 translations. Third came Stalin's writings with 689 translations. Tenth and eleventh on the list were Marx, with 415 translations, and Engels, with 409. The American writer highest on the list was Jack London, who stood fourteenth. None of the twenty-two American authors listed wrote explicitly on politics, economics, or religion.

Supplementing the "normal" informational channels of conventional governments, the Communists employ their special instruments—"Indigenous" Communist parties and Soviet-trained agitators and propagandists—for spreading both their basic ideology and their current foreign policy objectives. The Soviet Union is reported to be producing one hundred thousand trained propagandists and agitators a year. When Moscow gives the signal, this vast apparatus is set in motion to promote the Stockholm Peace Petition in 1950 or the campaign against nuclear weapon tests in 1957.

Since April 1949, the Soviet Union has been jamming the official Voice of America broadcasts beamed to her people. The Communists have also jammed Radio Free Europe, a privately-sponsored American effort, and selected international broadcasts of the British Broadcasting Corporation. After the Hungarian revolt of 1956, the Communist bloc strengthened its electronic curtain by intensifying its jamming of Western broadcasts. Monitors in Munich have traced more than one thousand Communists jamming transmitters, two hundred and fifty of which are located in East Germany alone. Some authorities estimate that the total cost of Communist jamming is more than one billion dollars a year. Voice of America officials in 1957 said that the Soviet Union was spending twice as much to jam Voice programs as it costs us to produce them.[4]

Soviet efforts at international persuasion are often regarded as moderately effective, at least in the short run, which is often long enough to serve their immediate objectives. Communist propaganda is especially effective in the "backward" areas of Asia and Africa where the memories of Western racism, economic exploitation, and colonialism are all too fresh. Soviet propaganda exploits these memories to the hilt. When the substantial sins of the West are measured against the insubstantial promises of Communism we get the worst of the bargain. And when our vices and Soviet virtues are both exaggerated, we don't seem to stand a chance, at least until some unvarnished facts about contemporary Communist and Western behavior come to the attention of persons only too eager to hear the worst about their former "oppressors." Of course, the Soviet Union occasionally makes life difficult for its professional propagandists by engineering a *coup d'état* in Czechoslovakia or by brutally suppressing a peoples' revolt in Hungary. One can only guess how much "good will," so patiently nurtured by the Communists in Asia over the previous decade, was lost because of the Budapest bloodbath.

We are concerned here not with the different assessments of the effectiveness of Soviet propaganda, but rather with the fact that these efforts, however effective or ineffective, do pose serious problems for the government of the United States, problems for which there are no adquate precedents.

From Psychological Warfare to International Information

Our government is a newcomer to the art of "psychological warfare." We did not take up the pursuit of this seemingly undemocratic and ungentlemanly craft until the necessities of World War II compelled us to do so, although in World War I we did have a brief but almost forgotten apprenticeship. During the early days of the last war most Americans were alternately repelled and fascinated by official plans "to plot the undoing of the psyches of their enemies," as Archibald Macleish once described the popular picture of "psychological warfare." [5]

Shortly after the outbreak of World War II, President Roosevelt recognized that the problem of pro-Nazi sympathies in Latin America was not unrelated to the national interests of the United States, so he assigned Nelson Rockefeller, his Coordinator of Inter-American Affairs, the additional task of supervising propaganda efforts to tell our story south of the border. In the spring of 1941 the President appointed Robert E. Sherwood as head of a new Foreign Information Service, and a year later the Office of War Information was established under the direction of Elmer Davis. By the end of the War we had enlisted some of the finest minds in the country in our propaganda effort. It was an entirely new experience for us, but we muddled through, learning a great deal from the British. Most observers conclude that we had a moderately effective program. Originally skeptical about the whole idea, General Eisenhower admitted in 1945 that "Psychological warfare has proved its right to a place of dignity in our military arsenal."

After the war we not only demobilized our troops, but we dismantled our propaganda apparatus as well. Psychological warfare may have been a military necessity, but we did not regard it as necessary or appropriate for the postwar period. The advent of the Cold War changed all this. We became increasingly aware that a clear statement of our objectives and policies was as essential in a cold war as in a shooting war. It was just as important to set the record straight in an international atmosphere poisoned by Radio Moscow after the war as it was to clear the air perfumed by Tokyo Rose and contaminated by Lord Haw Haw during the war. By 1948 the Soviet Union was engaged in a relentless campaign of vilification and falsehood against the United States and our Western allies. We could not assume that the peoples of Asia, the Middle East, Eastern Europe, or even of Western Europe would be able to distinguish the true from the false and see the United States and her foreign policies as they really were. Our problem was intensified by the fact that our new position of power and responsibility in the world increased the probability of suspicion, mistrust, and misunderstanding on the part of both allies and uncommitted nations. We had to be concerned about the accuracy of the image other peoples had of us.

Our legitimate concern to be seen abroad for what we really were could not be left to Hollywood films, to contacts with tourists, businessmen or missionaries, or to letters from relatives who had migrated to the United States. These contacts, which provided the major pre-World War II windows through which other peoples saw us, did not present a clear and adequate picture. During and since the war many peoples have seen us through our far-flung military forces or through governmental and private relief efforts. There were many voices of America, but there was no organized effort to explain our national purpose and how our foreign policies were related to it. Even well-organized private efforts such as Radio Free Europe, which were developed later and designed explicitly to correct the distorted image of the United States, could not do the over-all job that needed to be done.

It became clear that our government itself had to enter the picture in a deliberate and organized way, just as it had done in World War II, to supplement the many voices of America but not to suppress them. In 1948 reluctant members of Congress were persuaded by William Benton, then Assistant Secretary of State for Public Affairs, that international persuasion was as essential to the Cold War as "psychological warfare" had been during the Second World War. Congress authorized President Truman to appoint advisory commissions on International Information and Educational Exchange. Subsequently various programs in the area of international information and exchange were carried on under the State Department, and in 1953 the United States Information Agency was established as an independent office in the Executive Branch. The U.S.I.A. is to the wartime O.W.I. what the Marshall Plan was to the wartime Lend-Lease. Both Cold War agencies were established to carry on old tasks under new circumstances.

In performing its mission of dispensing American information and propaganda abroad, the U.S.I.A. as of 1957 had a staff of about twelve thousand and was spending approximately one hundred ten million dollars a year. Of this staff about 7,500 were foreign nationals employed in two hundred field offices in eighty-two foreign nations or territories. Of the some 4,300 Americans on the payroll, 1,500 were stationed abroad. The major services performed by the U.S.I.A. as of 1957 are 1) *Broadcasting:* The main activity consists of official Voice of America radio programs which are being transmitted in forty-five different languages for a total of 162 hours a week. The television service, begun in 1956, sends out films which are used in thirty-eight countries. 2) *Information Centers and Libraries:* There are 164 of these centers where American books, magazines, newspapers, and films are made available. The staffs of these centers answer questions about the United States, sponsor cultural and educational programs, and circulate films and exhibits. 3) *Press Service:* This service provides special materials, including the texts of official United States statements, to overseas U.S.I.A. centers and to the press of other nations. 4) *Motion Picture Service:* This service produces and acquires films depicting various aspects of American life for use abroad through commercial or U.S.I.A. channels.

Conflicting Views on International Persuasion

Any governmental program which sponsors such widely divergent activities as sending American jazz records to the Soviet Union, circulating a "People's Capitalism" exhibit in Asia, and providing free subscriptions to the *New York Times* and *New York Herald Tribune* for the 644 members of the British Parliament, is bound to be controversial. Each year Congress has to be persuaded anew that international persuasion is a good thing, or at least that the Information Agency was doing a good job of persuading. In April 1957 Senator Allen J. Ellender asserted that the U.S.I.A. has "grown like a bad weed," and called for a large cut in its proposed budget. President Eisenhower characterized the program as "America's voice of truth" and declared that to cut its budget would be "the worst kind of economy." Underlying the partisan differences in this annual battle of the budget are fundamentally conflicting views about what the United States should and should not do in the whole area of international information and persuasion.

Apart from a very small number of people who oppose all efforts in international propaganda, two major views have been expressed in Congress and in the public at large. The majority of Americans appear to support a substantial program of information which seeks to clarify abroad the image and foreign policy objectives of the United States. There is a vocal minority, however, who believe that this is not enough. This minority wants to expand the program from "information" to "ideology," from a small hundred-million-dollar voice to a mighty five-billion-dollar roar. They want a dynamic "Free World Ideology" to counteract and overcome Communist ideology. Our government's policies have for the most part been instructed by the informational school, but occasionally ideological overtones have found their way into official pronouncements.

Our Goal—"A Full and Fair Picture"

Most Americans would agree with Presidents Truman and Eisenhower that we need a substantial international information program to give other peoples a "full and fair picture" of the United States and her purposes, in order to correct innocent ignorance or deliberate distortion. In 1950, Mr. Truman called for a great "Campaign of Truth" to achieve this objective. His characterization of our propaganda efforts as a "campaign of truth" is somewhat pretentious and perhaps typically American. Two years later, on the occasion of the launching of the Voice of America transmitter ship *Courier,* Mr. Truman said that this ship "will be carrying a message of truth and light to those who are confused by the storm of falsehood that the Communists have loosed upon the world" and "will carry on the fight for freedom in the field where the ultimate victory will be won —that is, in the minds of men." President Eisenhower has also referred to our information program as a "campaign of truth," but neither Mr. Eisenhower nor Mr. Truman, despite their occasional use of crusading language, are really in the ideological school of international propaganda. They both have supported modest programs of factual information.

What our Government has actually meant by its "campaign of truth" has been elaborated in the more subdued and less poetic language of official directives. Two Presidential pronouncements in 1953 sum up the broad aims of the postwar propaganda program of the United States in these words: "The purpose of the United States Information Agency shall be to submit evidence to the peoples of other nations . . . that the objectives and policies of the United States are in harmony with and will advance their legitimate aspirations for freedom, progress and peace." This purpose is to be achieved by "explaining and interpreting . . . the objectives and policies of the United States Government," by presenting "imaginatively the correlation between United States policies and the legitimate aspirations of other peoples," by "unmasking and countering hostile attempts to distort or frustrate the objectives and policies of the United States," and by explaining "those important aspects of the life and culture" of the American people which will facilitate the understanding of the goals and policies of the United States. In another statement the President said that the "goals and desires which we hold in common must be explained in ways that will cause others to join with us in achieving them" and that "American broadcasts and printed materials should concentrate on factual news reporting, with particular selection and treatment of news designed to present a full exposition of United States actions and policies, especially as they affect the particular country addressed."

In carrying out these general purposes, the U.S.I.A. develops what it calls "global themes" or points of emphasis. Since it is obviously not possible to present a "full and fair picture" of the people, purposes and policies of the vast United States, our government focuses primarily on information which will clarify our foreign policy objectives. In May 1957 Arthur Larsen, director of the U.S.I.A., listed the four "global themes" then current as follows: 1) the United States is determined to unite "the free world in order to reduce the Communist threat without war," 2) the exposure of "the Communist Party or movement as a foreign force directed from Moscow or Peiping for expansionist purposes," 3) "the United States champions peace and progress through peaceful change," and 4) "the United States seeks, with other nations and peoples, to speed development and use of the atom for peace as a promise of a better life and a powerful force for world peace." [6] Doubts have been expressed about the effectiveness with which we were "getting across" these four points. Many observers believe that we were doing particularly poorly with the last one which deals with atomic energy.[7]

The "global themes" of our propaganda effort must be further tailored to meet the special needs of "target areas," which may be entire countries or elements of the population within a country. We do not need to convince the people of Hungary that Communist domination is bad or to tell the British that democracy is good. In broad terms, we seek to assure our allies that we are devoted to the common objectives that bind us together, that we understand their problems and respect their methods of dealing with them, and that we are dependable and constant. We seek to convince uncommitted nations that our aims are in harmony with their aspirations, and that Western Democracy has far more to offer them than does Soviet Communism. We attempt to discredit the objectives and methods of Soviet and Chinese Communism by citing the record. We try to persuade the captive nations of Eastern Europe that we are their true friends and that we look to the day when they will be free again; we try to give them hope without inciting premature revolt. We attempt to convince the Soviet Union that we are economically strong, militarily powerful, and morally resolute and that we are wedded indissolubly to our allies. These are difficult objectives to achieve, and we have often failed.

It may be useful to illustrate the technique of selecting information for a particular "target area" by recalling an incident which took place in Italy in 1951. In this case Italian Communists and Communist sympathizers were the target. The United States Information Staff in Rome produced a small handbill entitled *Per Una Pace Stabile* ("For a Lasting Peace"), designed to look exactly like a typical Communist handout. In addition to distributing a million copies of the leaflet through normal trade union channels, the U.S.I.A. had a bulk shipment of the leaflet delivered to a major Communist Party mailing room in northern Italy, where the well-disciplined faithful automatically sent out more than twenty thousand copies to the Party Membership list before they realized that they had been tricked into aiding "the enemies of Peace." The leaflet, whose sub-title was "25 Years of Soviet Efforts Toward Lasting Peace," listed a long series of international pledges which the Soviet Union has broken. Here are several examples from the list:

Pledge	*Result*
1925 — Turkish-Soviet Non-aggression Pact	The U.S.S.R. denounced this Pact in 1945.
1932 — Finnish-Soviet Non-aggression Pact	The U.S.S.R. invaded Finland in 1939.
1932 — Estonian-Soviet Non-aggression Pact	The U.S.S.R. annexed Estonia in 1940.
1932 — Polish-Soviet Non-aggression Pact	The U.S.S.R. seized Eastern Poland in 1939.
1937 — Chinese-Soviet Non-aggression Pact	In 1945 the Soviets plundered the industries of Manchuria.
1943 — Czech-Soviet Alliance	In 1948 a *coup d'état* supported by the Soviet Union reduced Czechoslovakia to a puppet of the U.S.S.R.
1945 — Yugoslavia-Soviet Alliance	The U.S.S.R. denounced this Alliance in 1949.

| 1945 — Polish-Soviet Alliance | In 1947 the Communists seized power in Poland, transforming that country into a Soviet puppet. |

The U.S.I.A. leaflet concluded with these words: "The Soviet Union has violated or denounced ten non-aggression or neutrality pacts in sixteen years. The Soviet Union has violated fourteen military alliances in thirteen years. When the Soviet Union talks about peace, remember these facts!" [8]

The Soviet suppression of the peoples' rebellion in Hungary in 1956 provided a mountain of grist for the American propaganda mill. It presented an unparalleled opportunity to expose Soviet Communism for what it is. Upon hearing the first confirmed reports of the Hungarian uprising, the U.S.I.A., according to an official report, covered developments on a "crash" basis. The Voice of America gave the story around-the-clock coverage. "During the first week, more than fifty per cent of all news broadcasts, which go out in forty-one foreign languages, plus English, were devoted to the Hungarian story. In news broadcasts to the people behind the Iron Curtain the percentage rose to sixty, then to eighty per cent." The other media of the Information Agency likewise were fully exploited. The story was told by word and picture throughout the world. "It seems probable that if this agency or a similar operation had not been in existence," said the U.S.I.A. report, "millions of people might never have learned the truth or might have heard only Communist distortions and lies about the revolution." [9]

The Limits of International Information

The most effective form of international persuasion is honest national self-disclosure, especially if our national character and purposes merit the respect of other peoples, but any foreign information program, even at its best, is subject to severe limitations. Propaganda is only one instrument of foreign policy, along with diplomacy, military force, and economic measures. Properly used international information can be a useful supplement to the other instruments of foreign policy, but it can never be a substitute for any one of them, much less a substitute for foreign policy itself. The attempt to substitute pronouncements or moralistic preachments for policy is bound to end in disaster. John Foster Dulles's article in *Life* magazine, "Policy of Boldness," [10] and other statements about liberating the captive peoples of Eastern Europe during the 1952 Presidential campaign led many Czechs, Hungarians, and Poles to believe that the United States would come to their aid in some tangible way in the event of an uprising.

Then came the Hungarian revolt in 1956. The United States did not act, and many fighters for freedom became bitterly disillusioned about our government. The fact that an unwarranted expectation seems to have been nourished more by the unofficial Radio Free Europe than by the official Voice of America, and that Mr. Dulles can "prove" that he never made any such promises by citing the fine print, does not change the larger fact that many people here and abroad are convinced that there was a serious and unjustified hiatus between pronouncement and policy, promise and performance. We spoke loudly and carried a small stick. Our policy of nonintervention in the Hungarian revolt was probably the only alternative open to us under the circumstances. Our response was criticized not because of the zeal with which we condemned the Soviet Union, but because many of the captive peoples were led to expect more than resolutions and pronouncements. This incident illustrates the dangers and limitations of propaganda, especially when it is motivated in part by the desire of American politicians to ingratiate themselves with certain groups of voters in the United States.

Our information program is an indispensable but limited handmaiden of foreign policy. The U.S.I.A. cannot and should not attempt to formulate national objectives or create national policies. Its primary task is to communicate the substance of the existing objectives and policies of the United States Government. If our country pursues a politically wise and morally responsible foreign policy, our information efforts can reflect these same qualities. If our overall foreign policy or particular policies are unwise and irresponsible, the problem cannot be solved by hiring a new set of publicity experts or sloganizers. The basic moral and political problem has to do with the substance of our national values and policies and not with the techniques employed to explain them to the world.

"Words at great moments of history are deeds," said Prime Minister Clement Attlee in praise of Winston Churchill whom he had just defeated at the polls in 1945. This is true only if words are backed up by deeds. Words can never be a substitute for deeds and are empty or dangerous without them. Churchill's words during the Battle of Britain were mighty because they were supported by the character, will, and determination of the British people. If words are empty without deeds, it is also true that deeds do not have their full impact without words. The deed is not complete until it is made known. The honest word about the deed is an appropriate extension of the deed. As long as the truth about the Battle of Budapest is made known through word and picture the courage and heroism of the deed will continue to live on.

The problem of relating political necessity to moral responsibility asserts itself on three levels as far as international persuasion is concerned. First, there is the problem of defining the national interest in terms broad enough to take into account the rights and legitimate interests of other peoples and thus merit their respect. Second, there is the problem of pursuing policies appropriate to this broader understanding of the national interest. And, third, there is the problem of making the national information effort an honest extension of the national purpose and national policies rather than permitting it to become a smokescreen for concealing or distorting national intentions. In this chapter we are concerned primarily with the third responsibility. Honest self-disclosure is not an easy task for a government which refers to its international propaganda program as a "Campaign of Truth" and at the same time promises a "full and fair picture" of those aspects of American life which will enable other peoples to understand our foreign policy objectives. Probably no responsible American official believes it is desirable or possible for any government to proclaim *The Truth,* which is, of course, an essentially religious task clearly beyond the capacity of governments and perhaps even of religious institutions, which *witness to* rather than *proclaim* ultimate truth.

What the government really means by the pretentious term "Campaign of Truth" is that we intend to give an honest and factual picture of those facets of American and Soviet life and behavior which we consider worth discussing. Even this more modest aim is not easy to achieve. Shall we report only our virtues and not our vices? Since we can deal with only a small number of facts, what shall be our basis for selecting the facts? Certainly we will want to tell the world about T.V.A., the Supreme Court decision outlawing segregation in public schools, and the success of the Marshall Plan. But shall we report the strident opposition to the Supreme Court decision, the ugly evidences of McCarthyism, and the hunger strikes among refugees in Austria against our restrictive immigration policies? If we really want to present an honest self-portrait, we must include a balanced reflection of our vices and virtues. For the most part this appears to have been the practice of our information program. In 1948 George V. Allen, then Assistant Secretary of State for Public Affairs, said: "The primary advantage we have over the propaganda efforts to totalitarian states today is the fact that we Americans are not obligated to present ourselves to the world as models of perfection. The United States has so many virtues to overcome its shortcomings that we need not fear the effect of our being truly known abroad. . . . In our information activity, we must present our civilization in its true color if we are to be effective. That color is gray—not lily-white." [11]

Honest national self-disclosure is dictated both by prudence and morality. If we do not report our vices with balance and proportion, we leave the field to the Soviet Union and other hostile governments which will report them with exaggeration and distortion. In the long run we have nothing to gain by pretending we are something we are not or that our policies will accomplish objectives they cannot accomplish. To be effective and morally defensible, international persuasion must be modest rather than boastful, restrained rather than strident. It is often said that the British habit of understatement, so eloquently illustrated in British Broadcasting Corporation broadcasts, is more effective than the less restrained tone of the Voice of America. The American tendency to overstatement is rooted deeply in our national character and cannot easily be corrected. A *New York Times* appraisal based upon a survey of U.S.I.A. activities in forty-four countries in 1952 concluded that, as a whole, the effectiveness of our information program had improved, but that "it is still too frequently obvious, boastful, and ostentatious." [12] The *Times* suggested that these shortcomings were a reflection of the American advertising mentality.

A distinction ought to be drawn between our broadcasting activities and our overseas Information Centers. Evidence suggests that these Centers, which contain American books, magazines, and newspapers, present a fuller and fairer picture of the United States than do Voice of America broadcasts, which tend to be geared to the news of the last twenty-four hours and are therefore more vulnerable to the impact of the recent and the sensational. Many official and unofficial observers have praised the quality of our U.S.I.A. Centers which, except for the short and shameful interlude of Cohn and Schine, have offered a balanced diet of American literature, news, and opinion.

Our accomplishments, our policies, our shortcomings speak more loudly than our words. If we want a more effective program of international persuasion, we must develop policies worthy of the respect of other nations and peoples. A powerful nation such as the United States will probably not be looked upon with affection or admiration, even by our close allies, but it is not beyond our capacity to earn the respect of friend, foe, and neutral if we follow a consistent and responsible foreign policy and if we explain this policy with modesty and restraint. There is a vast difference between being liked and being respected. Policies and pronouncements designed to engender the affection or approbation of a particular government or a people often invite scorn and disrespect. Policies worthy of respect, pursued with consistency and firmness, usually elicit respect.

"Marshall Plan of Ideas"

Since the end of World War II, a vocal minority in this country has been dissatisfied with the scope and magnitude of our government's information program. Some of these critics propose simply that the volumn of our program be greatly increased. Others insist that in addition to an increased volume of information the United States Government should launch an ideological crusade to combat the impact of Communism on the minds of men. Admiral Radford's program of "Militant Liberty" noted at the beginning of this chapter is almost wholly ideological in character. The two proposals which follow call for a greatly expanded information program and for a global ideological offensive.

In March 1950 Senator William Benton called upon the United States Government to launch a vigorous and "greatly expanded program of information and education among all the peoples of the world to the full extent that they can be reached—with a view to closing the mental gulf that separates the United States from other peoples and that now blockades the universal hope for freedom and peace" and urged that "the international propagation of the democratic creed be made an instrument of supreme national policy—by the development of a Marshall Plan in the field of ideas." The *New York Times* called Senator Benton's "Marshall Plan of Ideas" a "constructive" proposal and added: "We have the greatest idea in the world to 'sell' to people held in slavery—the idea of freedom—and the most alluring promise to offer—the promise of national independence and a decent living standard." [13] The *Washington Post* said: "It is high time the United States tried to capture leadership in the world of ideas in the manner Senator Benton has suggested." [14] Other comments of approval were less restrained, and some persons looked upon such an ideological offensive as a possible eventual alternative to military and economic measures.

In November 1950 George Gallup, director of the American Institute of Public Opinion, called for the creation of a new five-billion-dollar world-relations department in Washington to counteract the effect of Communist propaganda. Our present information program, he said, was trying "to convert millions of people to our point of view by sending out postcards of the Brooklyn Bridge." What we need, he held, is a bigger and better agency "staffed with the best brains of the country drawn from the fields of publishing, broadcasting, public relations, and advertising" which will be capable of presenting the values of American democracy to the masses abroad. Mr. Gallup said that the five billion dollars needed to launch his program could easily be obtained by reducing the current defense and foreign economic aid budgets by that amount. After certain minimum defense requirements are met, he said, "the safety and future of this nation can be insured to a greater extent by winning converts than by adding to our stock of arms" and after "we have given a certain amount of economic aid to other nations, additional amounts will not return the same increment of good will to us or strengthen our cause as much as the same amount of money spent in winning the minds of the people of these nations." [15]

The Dangers of an Ideological Crusade

The Radford, Benton, and Gallup proposals for launching a global psychological and ideological crusade have never been accepted by the State Department, the Congress, or the general public. This is a tribute to the good sense of the American people and their leaders. There are certain inescapable dangers in any aggressive national ideology, especially for a nation such as the United States which believes in and practices government by popular consent.

Advocates of an officially-sponsored ideological offensive tend to overlook the fact that ideology is but one element in the struggle between Soviet Communism and the free world and, what is more important, ideology is precisely the element which governments are least capable of dealing with. The Cold War, as far as foreign policy is concerned, is primarily a political, diplomatic, military, and economic struggle. Certainly ideas and loyalties are involved at every level of this struggle. But the objectives of a democratic foreign policy are and must be more modest than the objectives of national political religions such as Nazism and Communism. The central foreign policy goal of the United States today can be said to be the maintenance of our national independence, without war if possible, and the creation of an international climate where government by consent can flourish. In a vital conflict we would have to sacrifice the more inclusive values of this objective for the less inclusive values, because governments of nations have a primary moral responsibility for the security of their own people. "Winning the war in the minds of men" and "converting millions of people to our point of view" are lofty goals beyond the competence of any government. Dealing with the ultimate loyalty of men is essentially a religious and not a political question.

Proposals for a democratic ideology to counteract Communism embrace the rational-idealist illusion that to know the truth is to accept it. Religiously it can be said that the knowledge and acceptance of the Truth will make one free. Politically this is not true. We can preach the democratic gospel throughout the world, but it may have little impact on the ultimate loyalties of men, or even on their contingent political loyalties. Political loyalties are a product of many non-rational factors. Knowledge of the "democratic truth" alone will not insure that the possessor of that truth will become a democrat, much less a politically effective one. Political allegiance is the product of one's economic status, one's political environment, and one's total culture as well as one's religious values. Furthermore, the proclamation of political truth does not insure that it will be enthroned; to prevail in the political world truth must be backed by power. Education, even democratic education, will not remove international conflict, because conflict is rooted in the morally ambiguous nature of man. Does this mean that we should stop extolling the virtues of democracy? Hardly. It means only that we should not expect too much from preaching democracy and should turn our major attention to practicing it, and to the pursuit of foreign policies which respect the legitimate interests of all nations even though some of them may be undemocratic.

Crusading national ideologies with sweeping objectives tend to be expressions of national self-righteousness, or at least of the self-righteousness of the ruling elite. As such they fail to acknowledge the partiality and one-sidedness of the "truth" they proclaim. No man or nation can know, much less proclaim, the whole truth. Every man and nation is a mixture of truth and falsehood, vice and virtue. The crusading nation, in order to combat the half truth of another, is tempted to absolutize its own partial truth, making the nation into a god and demanding that contingent political loyalties become absolute religious loyalties. To recognize the contingent and relative character of men and nations is not to fall into the trap of saying that one man or one nation is just as good as the other. There are significant moral differences between the Communist world and the free world which dare not be overlooked. But the enemy's vices and our virtues may not be so exaggerated that the struggle becomes a simple crusade of the "good guys" against the "bad guys."

The temptation to moral and political oversimplification in any crusading ideology tend to lead to "holy" and unlimited wars. We tend to adopt the mood and psychology of the relatively simple shooting war to the vastly more complex Cold War. In a shooting war the overwhelming tangible objective is military victory, which calls for the military surrender of the enemy. In the Cold War the black-and-white contrasts of a shooting war give way to the subtle grays of a complex and many-sided struggle in which good and evil cannot be so absolutely identified. In 1934 William Graham Sumner said: "If you want a war, nourish a doctrine. Doctrines are the most frightful tyrants to which men ever are subject, because doctrines get inside of a man's own reason and betray him against himself." One need not accept Sumner's moral distinction between doctrine and reason to acknowledge the basic political truth of his statement, made just after Hitler had come to power. National political religions tend to lead to unlimited wars; they oversimplify the political and moral differences between the opposing camps and inspire in the faithful a religious zeal, a determination to give their all in the holy crusade to enthrone Truth over Error, Good over Evil, "Christian democracy" over "atheistic Communism." Ideological wars become total struggles between politically organized systems of self-righteousness. Compromise, adjustment, and negotiation, which are the very heart of diplomacy, become treason. "Unconditional surrender" of the enemy becomes the only acceptable objective.

The United States entered World War I to "make the world safe for democracy," and fought it with crusading zeal. There was less of the crusading mood in World War II and more of the "mournful warrior" mood, although we still insisted upon "unconditional surrender." The Korean War, like World War II, saw a mixture of moods among the American people. The temptation to adopt a crusading attitude toward the Soviet Union and World Communism is still disquietingly alive in the United States. We have our advocates of a "holy war," ideological or military, or both. And there is always a minority of our people ready to rally to a crusade for a "Free World ideology." Under certain conditions this minority could become the decisive majority.

CHAPTER SEVEN

*The American people most effectively exercise their
general control over foreign policy by choosing between alternative sets of political leaders rather than
by giving advice on day-by-day policy decisions.*

PAUL H. NITZE, 1956

THE PUBLIC AND FOREIGN
POLICY

In the fall of 1945, after the defeat of Germany and
Japan, the American people were weary of war.
Many of our citizens regarded World War II as a rude
interruption of their private peacetime pursuits. "We
have won the war. We have made our contribution
to international peace and decency. Now let's get
back to normal as quickly as possible." Sentiments
such as these were widespread. There were those,
of course, who insisted that the United States had a
continuing responsibility to maintain world peace and
security, but many of these "internationalists" believed
that somehow the United Nations would be a substitute for the heavy burdens of the new position of
power of the United States in the world. Both political "isolationists" and idealistic internationalists joined
in the chorus to "bring the boys home."

Some of President Truman's advisers warned him
against wholesale disarmament and demobilization.
They warned especially against the "point system"
which released first those men who had been longest

in the Armed Services, because it would destroy our strongest battle-tested units. The withdrawal of American power, they said, would weaken our position in Europe and Asia and invite Soviet power to fill the vacuum created by such a withdrawal. The President listened to the advice of the experts and seemed to agree with it, but felt he had to give in to the public pressure to "bring the boys home." To take up some of the slack caused by rapid demobilization, Mr. Truman advocated a program of Universal Military Training in the fall of 1945. The Congress, under fire from church and other anti-UMT pressure groups, did not give its consent even though opinion polls indicated that the majority of American citizens favored peacetime conscription.

Twelve years have passed. It would appear that the public and the Congress were wrong in their demands for drastic demobilization and that Mr. Truman's advisers were right. Perhaps it was politically impossible for the President to go against such strong public passion. Yet subsequent history has shown that our drastic demobilization, which had to be reversed even before the Korean War, served neither the national interests of the United States nor the larger values of international peace and security.

Mr. Truman was not the first President to go against his better judgment under powerful public pressure. His decision in 1945 recalls four earlier incidents in which the President and the State Department yielded to public passion and pursued foreign policies they opposed, and which subsequently were regarded as politically unwise and morally unjustifiable: McKinley going to war with Spain in 1898; Harding holding the Washington Disarmament Conference in 1921; Secretary Kellogg in 1928 negotiating the Paris Pact to "outlaw war"; and Roosevelt giving in to neutrality legislation in the 1930's. The last three policies, which contributed to the inevitability and magnitude of World War II, were demanded by organized pressure groups dedicated to a "warless world."

"The People Are Sovereign"

These examples of political leaders bowing to well-intentioned but ill-informed public pressure rather than serving the national interest as they understood it illustrate a dilemma faced by all democratic governments which, by definition, must take seriously the people in whose name they act and from whom they draw their power. Sir Harold Nicolson says: "In the days of the old diplomacy it would have been an act of unthinkable vulgarity to appeal to the common people upon any issue of international policy." But for Western democracies the old days are gone, and the people must be taken fully into account even if this means, as Hans J. Morgenthau suggests, "making foreign policy the hard way."

Walter Lippmann and other students of United States foreign policy, especially since the end of World War II, have been deeply concerned with the dilemma of the democratic statesmen. In 1955 Mr. Lippmann declared that "prevailing public opinion" in the United States "has been destructively wrong at the critical junctures" in United States foreign policy. "The people," he said, "have imposed a veto upon the judgments of informed and responsible officials. They have compelled the governments, which usually knew what would have been wiser, or was necessary, or was more expedient, to be too late with too little, or too long with too much, too pacifist in peace and too bellicose in war, too neutralist or appeasing in negotiation or too intransigent." This is true because "the cycle of subjective sentiments on war and peace is usually out of gear with the cycle of objective developments" and popular opinion reflects "a situation which no longer exists." [1]

Mr. Lippmann's charge that public opinion is ill-informed, tardy, and often wrong on international issues is shared by too many competent observers to be dismissed lightly. But it is not the whole story. The same "public" which in 1945 assumed that the United States had performed its duty for world peace by helping to crush totalitarianism and to establish the United Nations only two years later supported the Marshall Plan and military aid to Greece and Turkey, and in 1949 supported the creation of NATO. How could the same public be so wrong and so right about the international responsibilities of the United States? Under what conditions is public opinion a positive force in policy formation? When does it exert a negative influence?

Two Levels of Public Expression

The American people express what they believe about national issues on two levels. One level is usually designated by the term *public opinion*. Public opinion is the collective position of "the public," or, more accurately, articulate groups within the public, on issues of general concern. These issues may be broad or specific. The prevailing belief in the 1930's that the United States should stay out of Europe's affairs is an example of opinion on a broad issue. The view that the United States should not send an ambassador to the Vatican or should send wheat to India are examples of opinion on specific issues. Public opinion on current issues, whether they are general or specific, is always shifting, usually vague, often uninformed, always subject to irrational and irrelevant factors, and far more difficult to ascertain that Mr. George Gallup would have us believe.

On a deeper level the public expresses itself in terms of what it believes fundamentally about America and mankind. In Chapter One we spoke of those common values of freedom, justice, and fair play which most of our citizens believe in and which together define our purpose as a nation. This purpose is to preserve the United States as a free and democratic state and to pursue policies that will make for an international climate in which government by consent can flourish.

Public expression, both in terms of opinion on national issues and in terms of the national value consensus, plays an important role in the formulation and conduct of foreign policy. On the deeper level the national value consensus defines the limits within which the government must act and sets the goals which our leaders are morally obligated to pursue. Public expression on current foreign policy issues, as Mr. Lippmann points out, often involves demands which if yielded to would violate the general value consensus. In the late 1930's, for example, the American people were dedicated, and rightly so, to the preservation of the United States as a sovereign and democratic nation; but at the same time they insisted upon certain specific demands, including neutrality legislation, which made it almost impossible for President Roosevelt to honor their fundamental loyalties. The public did not realize it was making conflicting demands because it did not comprehend the realities of international politics.

When the immediate demands of the public or powerful pressure groups go against the long-term interests of the nation, the President finds himself in a difficult moral and political dilemma. George F. Kennan says that many of our unwise foreign policies have resulted from executive acquiescence to "short-term trends in public opinion." In situations in which the public fails to understand the nature and seriousness of a crisis, the policy makers, says Hans J. Morgenthau, "must either sacrifice what they consider good policy upon the altar of public opinion, or by devious means gain popular support for policies whose true nature they conceal from the public." [2] If public sentiment runs counter to the national purpose, a responsible President must either ignore this sentiment or seek to correct it by mobilizing support for his own policy proposals. If popular passion is too strong to ignore or correct, it appears that the two alternatives suggested by Mr. Morgenthau are the only ones left short of resigning from office.

The Limits of Public Advice on Specific Issues

There are four factors which limit the quality and effectiveness of public advice on current foreign policy issues.

1. *Public opinion is only one of the many factors which determine the foreign policy of a modern democratic state.* Foreign policy is largely the response of a national government to events and developments beyond the frontiers of its legal jurisdiction and, more important, beyond its capacity fully to control. This vast and stubborn external realm includes the power,

purpose, and unpredictability of hostile nations, allies and uncommitted peoples; the weight of tradition and precedent; the inexorable facts of international economic life; and the vicissitudes of history generally.

Among the internal factors which further narrow the foreign policy alternatives open to the government are the policy predisposition and resiliency of the party in power; the character and competence of the President and Secretary of State; the quality of the unending stream of advice and information from a multitude of experts in and out of government; the response of Congress; and, finally, "public opinion."

2. *Foreign policy problems are complex, delicate, and urgent.* Technical competence is required to understand the complexity of the great majority of international issues. Most problems involve delicate aspects which must remain confidential. On both counts direct participation by the public is ruled out. Even if all the important facets of a problem could be made public and the electorate had a much better understanding of the nature of world politics than it has, the rapidly changing international scene would usually force a decision long before the public could express an informed and relevant judgment.

3. *The Executive Branch of the United States Government has the primary responsibility for foreign policy; Congress plays a secondary role.* The President and the Executive Branch have the primary responsibility for the formulation of policy and the sole responsibility for administering it. Most policy proposals originate in the Executive Branch. The Congress can give or withhold its consent only on those matters prescribed by the Constitution. Through its control of the purse strings the Congress can veto or modify certain policies proposed by the President. On the majority of the most significant issues Congress for all

practical purposes is limited to expressing concurrence, but it can restrain the President directly by enacting laws designed to narrow the alternatives open to him. The neutrality laws of the 1930's and the unsuccessful efforts of Senator John W. Bricker from 1950 to 1957 to curb the President's treaty-making power by means of a Constitutional amendment are examples of Congressional attempts to restrain the Chief Executive. Congress tends to be least influential on major military-security issues and most influential on those nonsecurity questions which have specific domestic implications, such as immigration, tariffs, and foreign aid.

When Presidential leadership becomes weak, confused, or indecisive, Congress can and should increase its initiative in the formulation of foreign policy by boldly asserting its Constitutional prerogatives. Dean Acheson seemed to be calling for such initiative in January 1957, when he observed that in one "aspect of our foreign affairs Congress is all-powerful. This is in the establishing and maintaining of those fundamental policies, with their supporting programs of action, which require legal authority, men, and money. Without these foundations—solidly laid and kept in repair—even wise and skillful diplomacy cannot provide the power and develop the world environment indispensable to national independence and individual liberty for ourselves and others." [3]

4. *Certain persistent elements in the American character make it difficult for the public to form sound judgments on specific and current issues of national security.* Americans tend to want simple and permanent solutions to complex and continuing problems. We tend to see morally ambiguous problems in terms of moralistic black-and-white alternatives. Our mood, influenced by the slogans and over-simplifications of a none-too-responsible mass press, tends to fluctuate

from one extreme to the other. We tend to over-react to real or imagined danger and to be unduly apathetic in periods of stability and peace. Our preoccupation with "private values" and individual material success tends to blind us to the realities of world politics and make us insensitive to the interests of other peoples. Sometimes it takes a shock like Pearl Harbor or Korea to make us face up to international perils which statesmen and other experts had warned us about long before. Americans have a great capacity to respond with courage to danger and with compassion to need when the danger is clear and when the need is dramatic.

These four factors help to explain why it is difficult for the American public to have a direct and helpful impact on current foreign policy issues.

Lobbying—Effective and Ineffective

Members of the Executive Branch as well as Congressmen are acutely aware of public sentiment, and constantly take it into account. The State Department has an elaborate procedure for collecting and summarizing the results of public opinion polls and the views of church, educational, labor, business, veterans, and other groups for the information of top foreign policy makers. Everyone in Washington knows that major policies cannot succeed without public understanding and support. It is probably true to say, however, that the President, Secretary of State, or Congressman who is most dedicated to the national welfare is least influenced by the fluctuations in public sentiment and the advice of pressure groups on specific issues. This is as it should be. Senator John F. Kennedy said that the people of Massachusetts sent him to Washington not to "serve merely as a seismograph to record shifts in popular opinion." We Congressmen, he continued, have been selected by the voters because they had "confidence in our judgment and our ability" to serve the nation's interests. "This may mean that we on occasion lead, inform, correct, and sometimes even ignore constituent opinion." [4]

Most pressure groups, because of their institutional self-interest or an inadequate understanding of world politics, are unable to see foreign policy issues in all their depth, breadth, and complexity. Consequently, their advice is usually wrong or irrelevant. Lobbyists almost always focus on specific problems of special concern to their organization. The religious, peace, and other pressure groups which have lobbied against Universal Military Training during the past fifteen years, for example, constantly condemned the "evils" of peacetime military training, but they seldom if ever came to grips with the problem of comparing the evils of UMT with the evils of alternative means of maintaining the same posture of national defense. These groups succeeded in blocking what many students of the problem believe to be the manpower program most compatible with our democratic values. We are not debating the merits of UMT here, but simply noting that pressure groups opposing a specific policy often fail to take into account the consequences of alternative policies, one of which will have to be adopted if their efforts succeed. A statesman who seeks to honor the values of the public must assess the probable consequences of alternative policies and must choose one policy over another. He never enjoys the luxury of simply opposing one alternative. Further, he has to face public criticism or loss of office if his choice is subsequently judged by the majority to be unwise or wrong.

On relatively simple and morally clear-cut issues, such as immigration questions or famine relief, voluntary pressure groups often make a positive contribution to foreign policy by urging the better of two alternatives upon reluctant policy makers. For instance, the pressure of church groups helped Congress to pass the $190,000,000 grain-to-India bill in 1951.

Organizations with special competence in certain problems can also be helpful to policy makers. One of the best examples of a technically competent group is the Committee for Economic Development, a business organization which prepares scholarly reports on domestic and foreign economic questions. Occasionally the Committee testifies before a Congressional committee. Its reports and recommendations are widely respected by our government and by the business world. The studies of the Council on Foreign Relations and the American Political Science Association are also highly respected. Unfortunately there is little lobbying by groups having the level of specialized competence of these organizations.

Religious and other morally concerned groups could have a more significant and positive impact on foreign policy if they engaged in a kind of lobbying somewhat different from their usual approach. Recognizing that they are limited in the technical competence required to speak helpfully on most specific questions, they could perform a valuable service by reminding our policy makers of our common values, insisting that Congress and the Administration justify their policy decisions and recommendations in terms of these values.

Take Universal Military Training, for example. Members of Congress and officials in the Executive

Branch who deal with questions of defense and manpower might well be reminded of six major values held by the overwhelming majority of the American people which relate to this issue. Any manpower program should 1) provide the level of defense required, 2) be operated as economically as possible, 3) produce the least possible disruption in the educational and vocational plans of the men involved, 4) be as free as possible from psychological or ideological regimentation, 5) embody the democratic principle of equally shared responsibility, and 6) honor the right of citizens to be conscientious objectors. Obviously these values cannot all be realized fully; some tend to conflict with others. But they all need to be kept in mind because of the constant temptation to make decisions primarily in terms of a single value. Instead of concentrating their concern almost exclusively on the issue of regimentation, religious church groups would have made a more positive contribution to the problem had they insisted that the proponents of various manpower proposals justify their proposals on all six counts.

The primary responsibility of morally-conscious *citizens and voluntary groups* is to uphold and clarify the basic values of our society. The duty of *experts and specialists* in and out of government is to study complex questions of foreign policy, to suggest alternative means of dealing with them, and to make known the probable consequences of various alternatives. The responsibility of our *policy makers* is to choose and carry out those policies which they believe will best serve our common national objectives and values. Groups which understand the respective roles of these three elements in foreign policy formation can make a genuine contribution to sound policies in Washington by helping legislators and administrators to pursue policies which honor our highest values. Some church pronouncements on foreign policy questions have embraced this understanding, and some church lobbying has taken place on this level. But even this effective form of representation in Washington is not the primary way the electorate influences the direction and quality of our foreign policy.

How "the Public" Is Most Effective

The American people do determine the behavior of the United States in world politics. Our foreign policy may exhibit varying degrees of responsibility, but ultimately it is in the hands of "the people" and it will remain there as long as our free political institutions continue to function. Adult citizens make their basic contribution to foreign policy *not* by giving advice on day-by-day policy decisions, but by determining the values for which this nation stands, by creating a climate in which these values can effectively be pursued, and by choosing between alternative sets of leaders to run the government.

1. *The public determines the national purpose:* In our homes, schools, and churches the values which make up our national purpose are transmitted, renewed, and reinterpreted. It is the duty of the President, in consultation with his advisers and with the consent of Congress, to translate this purpose into appropriate policies. In 1947, for example, President Truman proposed that our national goals of peace and security could best be served by active United States leadership in a free-world coalition. Public support for Mr. Truman's foreign policy was registered in Congressional appropriations for the Marshall Plan

and for economic and military aid to Greece and Turkey, and in the results of the 1948 election. Public opinion on current issues is most reliable when it is a positive response to the decisive leadership of a President who has the humility to learn from the wisdom of the people and the courage to ignore the foolishness of their passing passions.

2. *The public creates the psychological and moral climate in which foreign policy is formulated and conducted.* When the national atmosphere is poisoned by exaggerated fears or illusory hopes, responsible public debate and decision becomes difficult or impossible. To fear real danger is prudence; to be frightened by imaginary perils is hysteria. Unwarranted optimism also creates a climate in which our leaders cannot make the hard decisions required by the tragedies and contingencies of world politics. Many observers here and abroad have accused Secretary of State Dulles of sponsoring false optimism, especially in the years 1955 and 1956. On August 26, 1955, for example, Mr. Dulles said this: "One of the first things I did as Secretary of State was to go to the Middle East. . . . At that time the Suez base was a center of controversy and potential strife. Now, as a result of patient effort, in a spirit of conciliation, the problem of the Suez base has been successfully resolved." The *Manchester Guardian* likened Mr. Dulles' "unreal" world to "a morality play acted by puppets." The easiest way for a Secretary of State to make his difficult job more difficult is to encourage a false optimism about international problems, a mood which would most certainly undercut any stern measures he should subsequently feel compelled to take. The quality of the national moral climate is determined by many factors, including the moral health of the school, the church, and the media of mass communication, and the extent to which our life as a nation corresponds

to the values we profess. Our racial discrimination and our discriminatory immigration laws and practices have compromised the integrity of our national character and have hurt us abroad.

3. *The public translates its will into national policy chiefly through the two-party system.* Choosing between the Republican and Democratic parties is the electorate's most effective means of influencing the direction and quality of United States foreign policy. Professor E. E. Schattschneider says that "the existing party structures are the greatest multipliers and amplifiers of political energy ever invented." Through a major party the voters deal with many of the most important issues simultaneously. Each party has a general policy predisposition on a great variety of domestic and foreign policy issues which citizens could never deal with one by one. Both the Republican and Democratic parties reflect the general moral and political consensus of the American people, but there is a persistent and predictable marginal difference on many issues which gives the voter a genuine opportunity to influence the character of foreign policy. It is far more important to get the more responsible candidate or the more responsible party in office than it is to attempt to influence the wrong candidate or the wrong party after the election. A thousand letters to the late Senator McCarthy urging him to respect human rights probably would not have moved him an inch, but a slight shift of votes in Wisconsin in 1952 would have moved him a thousand miles.

The President and the Public

The President takes an oath to defend the United States and the values for which our nation stands. Often there is a serious conflict between foreign policy measures which honor these values and the immediate demands and expectations of large segments of the public. What should a morally-responsible President and his advisers do? Certainly they dare not give in to public passion and thereby sell short the public interest. Paul H. Nitze, former director of the State Department Policy Planning Staff, puts it this way: "When our political leaders look to the public for guidance on tactical issues, or even on matters of strategy, I think they err and are delinquent in their duty. When they ignore the essential underlying values of the people in the formulation of strategy, or in deciding on specific tactics, I think they err even more seriously."

The principle of giving priority to the fundamental values of the people over their current opinions is clear, but it is difficult to apply in the real world of practical politics where national decisions must be made. There appears to be no solution short of strong executive leadership. Hans J. Morgenthau says that "the government must realize that it is the leader and not the slave of public opinion; that public opinion is not a static thing to be discovered and classified by public-opinion polls as plants are by botanists, but that it is a dynamic, ever-changing entity to be continuously created and recreated by informed and responsible leaderships." [5] In order to lead effectively, the President and Secretary of State must be patient. They must recognize that there is no way for the public to keep its traditional values in good repair without discussing, arguing over, and to some extent interfering in day-by-day foreign policy issues. Our leaders must also distinguish between essential and less-than-essential issues and be willing to compromise with public sentiment on the less-than-essential matters. They must fight for the essentials. In doing this they help to raise the general level of public understanding and make it less difficult to pursue sound policies in the future. If, however, a President is unable to muster adequate support for his minimum program which he believed to be essential to the security of the country, he will either have to pursue his policies by resorting to a measure of manipulation or deceit or resign from his high office.

When the American people understand that certain matters are the responsibility of the President and the Executive Branch and certain other matters are the responsibility of the public, a more wholesome and effective relationship between the government and the people will result. The Congress, the Executive Branch, and foreign policy specialists in and out of government are instruments through which the values of the public are related to the problems of international politics. The public makes the most effective use of these instruments, not by offering advice on day-by-day issues, but by renewing and clarifying the values for which the nation stands, by creating a climate in which these values can be effectively pursued, by insisting that the government adopt policies appropriate to our values, and by choosing between alternative sets of leaders to govern the country.

The Contribution of the Church and Synagogue

Since 1900 the churches and synagogues of the United States have issued thousands of pronouncements on questions of foreign policy. Their accredited representatives have gone to Washington thousands of times to present views to the President, the Secretary of State, or the Congress. Most competent observers believe that the influence of church pronouncements and direct lobbying on the direction of foreign policy has not been great. In those cases where church lobbying was effective, the policies advocated very often turned out to be unsound.

On a deeper level the churches have made a significant and positive contribution to United States foreign policy. Along with the home and the school, the churches have been the custodians and interpreters of our deepest values. Generations of our citizens have been brought up under the social teachings of Judaism and Christianity. Our preachers, priests, and rabbis have talked about peace, justice, good will, and the sovereignty of a God who knows no favorites among the nations. The social message of the churches was often presented in terms of ideal goals which seemed to bear little relation to the realities of world politics, and this message was usually not accompanied by a full understanding of the limits and possibilities of human nature and history.

While it is true that utopianism and moralism have dominated the foreign policy views of the most vocal churchmen in the United States since the turn of the century, it is also true that the churches have done a better job than they knew. Many of our political leaders have been motivated by the central values and insights of the Judaeo-Christian tradition which somehow managed to get through the defensive shield of nineteenth-century liberal idealism. Some of these men have been morally sensitive and politically wise enough to see the relevance of the "ideal ends" of the preacher to the limited means of the politician. They have learned the art of relating ethics to political necessity without slipping into moral pretension on the one side of cynicism on the other. The churches have prepared men with enough courage to reject the specific foreign policy advice of the churches precisely because of their loyalty to what the churches fundamentally stand for. These statesmen have been better able to relate the wisdom of the Judaeo-Christian heritage to the tragic realm of politics than most professional churchmen because the statesmen had been disciplined by a more profound understanding of history and chastened by political responsibility. The high ideals of the churchmen were frequently not qualified either by political wisdom or a genuine understanding of Biblical religion.

In the past decade an increasing number of religious leaders in the United States have been rejecting the earlier optimism about man and the world. With this shift toward "Biblical realism" there has come a greater understanding of the nature of world politics and foreign policy and a greater appreciation for the contribution of scholars, statesmen, and other specialists to the problems of political ethics. With this greater understanding has come a more effective witness on the part of the churches in this fateful age when "America's foreign policy is everybody's destiny."

BIBLIOGRAPHY

There has been very little serious writing which explicitly relates Judaeo-Christian ethics to the formulation and conduct of United States foreign policy. The many books and articles written by Reinhold Niebuhr over the past three decades are the major exception. This selected bibliography is designed to include the best available essays on ethics and foreign policy as well as other serious essays which deal with the various aspects of United States foreign policy treated in the present work. For the general reader the two volumes of readings listed at the head of this bibliography are probably the most valuable single sources. The remaining titles are arranged alphabetically by author.

* GORDON, MORTON AND VINES, KENNETH N., editors. *Theory and Practice of American Foreign Policy*. New York: Thomas Y. Crowell, 1955.

   See especially Kenneth W. Thompson, "Theories of

International Political Behavior," pages 10-17 and the entire section, "The American Approach to International Politics," pages 18-149. In addition to essays by scholars, this book includes selections from George Washington, Thomas Jefferson, Woodrow Wilson, Herbert Hoover, Franklin D. Roosevelt, Harry S. Truman, Dwight D. Eisenhower, George C. Marshall, Dean Acheson, John Foster Dulles, George F. Kennan and Charles E. Bohlen.

* MORGENTHAU, HANS J. AND THOMPSON, KENNETH W., editors. *Principles and Problems of International Politics.* New York: Alfred A. Knopf, 1950.

In addition to essays from American statesmen and scholars this book includes selections from Sir Winston Churchill, Lord Salisbury, Edmund Burke, Prince de Talleyrand, David Hume and others.

ACHESON, DEAN. *A Citizen Looks at Congress.* New York: Harper & Brothers, 1957.

ACHESON, DEAN. *A Democrat Looks at His Party.* New York: Harper & Brothers, 1955.

ALMOND, GABRIEL A. *The American People and Foreign Policy.* New York: Harcourt, Brace and Co., 1950.

ALMOND, GABRIEL A. *The Appeals of Communism.* Princeton: Princeton University Press, 1954.

BARGHOORN, FREDERICK C. *The Soviet Image of the United States.* New York: Harcourt, Brace and Co., 1950.

BARRETT, EDWARD W. *Truth Is Our Weapon.* New York: Funk & Wagnalls Co., 1953.

BECKER, CARL L. *How New Will the Better World Be?* New York: Alfred A. Knopf, 1944.

BEMIS, SAMUEL FLAGG. *A Diplomatic History of the United States.* Third Edition. New York: Henry Holt and Co., 1950.

BENNETT, JOHN C. *Communism and the West: the Basic Conflicts.* New York: Church Peace Union, 1953.

BOORSTIN, DANIEL J. *The Genius of American Politics.* Chicago: University of Chicago Press, 1953.

BOWLES, CHESTER. *The New Dimensions of Peace*. New York: Harper & Brothers, 1955.

BRIERLY, J. L. *The Law of Nations*. 4th ed; Oxford: The Clarendon Press, 1942.

BRIERLY, J. L. *The Outlook for International Law*. Oxford: The Clarendon Press, 1944.

BUNDY, MCGEORGE, editor. *The Pattern of Responsibility*. Boston: Houghton Mifflin Co., 1951.

> The record of Secretary of State Acheson from January 1949 to August 1951 drawn largely from the words of Mr. Acheson in speeches, articles and official documents.

BUZZARD, SIR ANTHONY W. "Massive Retaliation and Graduated Deterrence," *World Politics*, January, 1956, pages 228-237.

CARR, EDWARD HALLETT. *The Twenty Years' Crisis: 1919-1939*. Second Edition. London: Macmillan, 1946.

COMMITTEE FOR ECONOMIC DEVELOPMENT. *Economic Development Assistance*. April 1957.

DAHL, ROBERT A. *Congress and Foreign Policy*. New York: Harcourt, Brace and Co., 1950.

DAVIS, ELMER. "Vox Populi and Foreign Policy," *Harper's Magazine*, June, 1952, pages 66-73.

DESCHWEINITZ, KARL, JR. and THOMPSON, KENNETH W. *Man and Modern Society*. New York: Henry Holt & Co., 1953.

DULLES, JOHN FOSTER. "A Righteous Faith," *Life*, December 28, 1942, pages 49-51.

DULLES, JOHN FOSTER. "Policy for Security and Peace," *Foreign Affairs*, April, 1954, pages 353-364.

DULLES, JOHN FOSTER. "Policy of Boldness," *Life*, May 19, 1952, pages 146 following.

DULLES, JOHN FOSTER. *War or Peace*. New York: Macmillan Co., 1950.

DUNN, FREDERICK S. *War and the Minds of Men*. Published for Council on Foreign Relations by Harper & Brothers, New York, 1950.

FOSDICK, DOROTHY. *Common Sense and World Affairs*. New York: Harcourt, Brace and Co., 1955.

FOX, WILLIAM T. R. "Interwar International Relations Research: the American Experience," *World Politics,* October, 1949, pages 67-79.

FOX, WILLIAM T. R. *The Super-Powers.* New York: Harcourt, Brace and Co., 1944.

FOX, WILLIAM T. R. "The United Nations in an Era of Total Diplomacy," *International Organization,* Vol. 5, No. 2, 1951.

HALLE, LOUIS J. *Civilization and Foreign Policy.* New York: Harper & Brothers, 1955.

HERZ, JOHN H. *Political Realism and Political Idealism.* Chicago: University of Chicago Press, 1951.

HOFFMAN, PAUL G. "Blueprint for Foreign Aid," *New York Times Magazine,* February 17, 1957, pages 9 following.

HOLLOWAY, VERNON H. "Utopianism and Realism in Foreign Policy," in *Christian Faith and Social Action* edited by John A. Hutchison. New York: Charles Scribner's Sons, 1953, pages 175-198.

HOTZ, ALFRED J. *The United Nations: New Perspectives.* New York: The Church Peace Union, 1955.

JONES, JOSEPH M. *The Fifteen Weeks.* New York: Viking Press, 1955.

KAUFMANN, WILLIAM W., editor. *Military Policy and National Security.* Princeton: Princeton University Press, 1956.
    See especially "The Requirements of Deterrence," by William W. Kaufmann, pages 12-38.

KEGLEY, CHARLES W. and BRETALL, ROBERT W., editors. *Reinhold Niebuhr: His Religious, Social and Political Thought.* New York: Macmillan Co., 1956.
    See especially "Reinhold Niebuhr's Role in American Political Thought and Life" by Arthur Schlesinger, Jr., pages 126-150, and "The Political Philosophy of Reinhold Niebuhr" by Kenneth W. Thompson, pages 152-175.

KENNAN, GEORGE F. *American Diplomacy: 1900-1950.* Chicago: University of Chicago Press, 1951.

KENNAN, GEORGE F. *Realities of American Foreign Policy.* Princeton: Princeton University Press, 1954.

KENNAN, GEORGE F. "Training for Statesmanship," *The Atlantic Monthly,* May, 1953, pages 40-43.

KISSINGER, HENRY A. *Nuclear Weapons and Foreign Policy.* New York: Harper & Brothers, 1957.

LASSWELL, HAROLD D. *Propaganda Technique in the World War.* New York: Alfred A. Knopf, 1927.

LEFEVER, ERNEST W. "Evanston on International Affairs," *Christianity and Crisis,* November 29, 1954, pages 158-160.

LINEBARGER, PAUL M. A. *Psychological Warfare.* Washington: Infantry Journal Press, 1948.

LIPPMANN, WALTER. *The Cold War.* New York: Harper & Brothers, 1947.

LIPPMANN, WALTER. *Isolation and Alliances: An American Speaks to the British.* Boston: Little, Brown and Co., 1952.

LIPPMANN, WALTER. *The Public Philosophy.* Boston: Little, Brown and Co., 1955.

LIPPMANN, WALTER. *U. S. Foreign Policy: Shield of the Republic.* Boston: Little, Brown and Co., 1943.

MARSHALL, CHARLES BURTON. *The Limits of Foreign Policy.* New York: Henry Holt and Co., 1954.

MILLER, WILLIAM LEE. "The Irony of Reinhold Niebuhr," *The Reporter,* January 13, 1955, pages 11-15.

MILLER, WILLIAM LEE. "The 'Moral Force' Behind Dulles's Diplomacy," *The Reporter,* August 9, 1956, pages 17-20.

MORGENTHAU, HANS J. "The Decline and Fall of American Foreign Policy," *New Republic,* December 10, 1956, pages 11-16 and December 17, 1956, pages 14-18.

MORGENTHAU, HANS J. *In Defense of the National Interest.* New York: Alfred A. Knopf, 1951.

MORGENTHAU, HANS J. *Politics Among Nations.* Second Edition. New York: Alfred A. Knopf, 1954.

MORGENTHAU, HANS J. *Scientific Man vs. Power Politics.* Chicago: University of Chicago Press, 1946.

MORGENTHAU, HANS J. and FOX, WILLIAM T. R. "National Interest and Moral Principle in Foreign Policy," *American Scholar,* Spring, 1949, pages 207-215.

NICOLSON, HAROLD. *Diplomacy.* Second Edition. London: Oxford University Press, 1950.

NICOLSON, HAROLD. *The Evolution of Diplomatic Method.* New York: Macmillan Co., 1955.

NICOLSON, HAROLD. "The Faults of American Diplomacy," *Harper's Magazine,* January, 1955, pages 52-58.

NIEBUHR, REINHOLD. *America's Spiritual Resources for International Cooperation.* Washington: U. S. National Commission for UNESCO, 1955.

NIEBUHR, REINHOLD. *The Children of Light and the Children of Darkness.* New York: Charles Scribner's Sons, 1944.

See especially pages ix-xiii and 153-190.

NIEBUHR, REINHOLD. *Christian Realism and Political Problems.* New York: Charles Scribner's Sons, 1953.

See especially "The Illusion of World Government," pages 15-31, and "The Foreign Policy of American Conservatism and Liberalism," pages 53-73.

NIEBUHR, REINHOLD. *Christianity and Power Politics.* New York: Charles Scribner's Sons, 1940.

NIEBUHR, REINHOLD. "Democracy as a Religion," *Christianity and Crisis,* August 4, 1947, pages 1-2.

NIEBUHR, REINHOLD. *The Irony of American History.* New York: Charles Scribner's Sons, 1952.

NIEBUHR, REINHOLD. *The Moral Implications of Loyalty to the United Nations.* New Haven, Conn.: Edward Hazen Foundation, 1952.

NIEBUHR, REINHOLD. *Moral Man and Immoral Society.* New York: Charles Scribner's Sons, 1932.

See especially pages xi-xxv and "The Morality of Nations," pages 83-112.

NIEBUHR, REINHOLD. "Peace Through Cultural Cooperation," *Christianity and Crisis,* October 17, 1949, pages 131-133.

NIEBUHR, REINHOLD. "Politics and the Christian Ethic," *Christianity and Society,* Spring, 1940, pages 24-28.

NIEBUHR, REINHOLD. *Reflections on the End of An Era.* New York: Charles Scribner's Sons, 1934.

See especially "The Political Realism of Christian Orthodoxy," pages 207-225, and "The Balance of Power in Politics," 243-248.

NITZE, PAUL H. "Atoms, Strategy and Policy," *Foreign Affairs,* January, 1956, pages 187-198.

NITZE, PAUL H. " 'Impossible' Job of Secretary of State,"

New York Times Magazine, February 12, 1957, pages 9 following.

NITZE, PAUL H. "The Modern President As a World Figure," *Annals of the American Academy of Political and Social Science,* September, 1956, pages 114-123.

NITZE, PAUL H. *U. S. Foreign Policy: 1945-1955.* New York: Foreign Policy Association, 1956.

OSGOOD, ROBERT ENDICOTT. *Ideals and Self-Interest in America's Foreign Relations.* Chicago: University of Chicago Press, 1953.

OSGOOD, ROBERT ENDICOTT. *Limited War: The Challenge to American Strategy.* Chicago: University of Chicago Press, 1957.

PEARSON, LESTER B. *Democracy in World Politics.* Princeton: Princeton University Press, 1955.

Representation of The United States Abroad, The. A report of The American Assembly, Graduate School of Business, Columbia University, June 1956.

ROBERTS, HENRY L. *Russia and America: Dangers and Prospects.* New York: Published for the Council on Foreign Relations by Harper & Brothers, 1956.

SNYDER, RICHARD C. and FURNISS, EDGAR S., JR. *American Foreign Policy.* New York: Rinehart & Co., 1954.

STALEY, EUGENE. *The Future of Underdeveloped Countries:* Political Implications of Economic Development. New York: Published for the Council on Foreign Relations by Harper & Brothers, 1954.

STEPHENS, OREN. *Facts to a Candid World: America's Overseas Information Program.* Stanford, Stanford University Press, 1955.

STEVENSON, ADLAI. *Call To Greatness.* New York: Harper & Brothers, 1954.

THOMPSON, KENNETH W. "Collective Security Reexamined," *American Political Science Review,* September, 1953, pages 753-772.

THOMPSON, KENNETH W. "Toward A Theory of International Politics," *American Political Science Review,* September, 1955, pages 733-746.

THORP, WILLARD L. *Trade, Aid or What?* Baltimore: John Hopkins Press, 1954.

DE TOCQUEVILLE, ALEXIS. *Democracy in America.* Two Volumes. New York: Alfred A. Knopf, 1945.

WARD, BARBARA. *Faith and Freedom.* New York: Norton, 1954.

WOLFERS, ARNOLD. " 'National Security' As An Ambiguous Symbol," *Political Science Quarterly,* December, 1952, pages 481-502.

WOLFERS, ARNOLD and MARTIN, LAURENCE W., editors. *The Anglo-American Tradition in Foreign Affairs:* Readings from Thomas More to Woodrow Wilson. New Haven: Yale University Press, 1956.

NOTES

ETHICS AND INTERNATIONAL POLITICS

[1] *The Irony of American History:* New York, Scribner's, 1952, p. viii.
[2] Professor Hans J. Morgenthau, Letter to the *New York Times,* November 13, 1956.
[3] *New York Post,* November 23, 1943.
[4] The relation of "the public" to foreign policy is dealt with in Chapter Seven.
[5] *The Children of Light and the Children of Darkness,* New York, Scribner's, 1944, p. xi.
[6] "Training for Statesmanship," *The Atlantic Monthly,* May 1953, pp. 40-43.
[7] *Scientific Man vs. Power Politics:* University of Chicago Press, 1946, p. 203.
[8] For a helpful discussion on American approaches to foreign policy see Kenneth W. Thompson, "Theories of International Political Behavior," in *Theory and Practice of American Foreign Policy* by Morton Gordon and Kenneth N. Vines: New York, Thomas Y. Crowell, 1955, pp. 10-17.

PEACE, SECURITY AND THE COLD WAR

[1] Quoted in the *New York Times,* November 18, 1955.
[2] The relation of the United States to the United Nations will be discussed in Chapter 4.

[3] *New York Times Magazine,* October 18, 1953.

[4] This point is elaborated in Chapter 5.

[5] See *The Fifteen Weeks* by Joseph M. Jones: New York, Viking Press, 1955.

[6] The limits and possibilities of the United Nations are discussed in Chapter 4.

[7] *New York Times,* December 25, 1955.

[8] See Paul H. Nitze, "Atoms, Strategy and Policy," *Foreign Affairs,* January 1956, pp. 187-198, and Sir Anthony W. Buzzard, "Massive Retaliation and Graduated Deterrence," *World Politics,* January 1956, pp. 228-237. The best new book on this subject is Henry A. Kissinger, *Nuclear Weapons and Foreign Policy:* New York, Harper, 1957.

THE DILEMMA OF DEMOCRATIC DIPLOMACY

[1] For a remarkably forthright official statement on this subject see Charles E. Bohlen, "Negotiation from Strength," in *Theory and Practice of American Foreign Policy* by Morton Gordon and Kenneth N. Vines: New York, Thomas Y. Crowell, 1955, pp. 430-438. The essay originally appeared in the *State Department Bulletin,* August 4, 1952.

[2] The problem of ideology will be dealt with at greater length in Chapter 6.

[3] See James Reston, "A Policy Boomerangs," *New York Times,* February 4, 1957.

[4] "Ethics and Foreign Policy," *World Alliance News-Letter,* Church Peace Union, October 1956, pp. 4 and 5.

[5] "An Open Look at Secret Diplomacy," *New York Times Magazine,* September 13, 1953, p. 47.

[6] Letter from Wilson to Secretary of State Robert Lansing, June 12, 1918.

[7] The relation of the public and Congress to foreign policy is discussed in detail in Chapter 7.

[7a] *Ibid.*

[8] "An Open Look at Secret Diplomacy," *op. cit.,* p. 48.

[9] *Washington Post and Times Herald,* December 29, 1956.

[10] "The Faults of American Diplomacy," *Harper's Magazine,* January 1955, p. 50.

[11] *Washington Post and Times Herald,* February 1, 1957.

[12] *Ibid.,* March 22, 1957.

[13] See Paul H. Nitze, " 'Impossible' Job of Secretary of State," *New York Times Magazine,* February 12, 1957.

[14] *Parliamentary Debates,* House of Commons, London, v. 446, no. 48, pp. 562-563.

THE UNITED NATIONS—INSTRUMENT OF NATIONAL POLICY

[1] For two Protestant critiques of Dulles, see John C. Bennett, "John Foster Dulles," *Christianity and Society,* Winter 1952-1953, pp. 4, 5; William Lee Miller, "The 'Moral Force' Behind Dulles's Diplomacy," *The Reporter,* August 9, 1956, pp. 17-20.

[2] See Hans J. Morgenthau, "The Decline and Fall of American Foreign Policy," *New Republic,* December 10, 1956, pp. 11-16.

[3] *Christianity and Society,* Winter 1952-1953, p. 3.

[4] *Washington Post and Times Herald,* February 7, 1957.

[5] *Ibid.*

[6] *Ibid.,* February 8, 1957.

[7] See Reinhold Niebuhr, "Peace Through Cultural Cooperation," *Christianity and Crisis,* October 17, 1949, pp. 131-133.

[8] See Chapter 3 for a discussion of the limitations of "conference" and "public" diplomacy.

[9] See Reinhold Niebuhr, "The Illusion of World Government," *Foreign Affairs,* April 1949, pp. 379-388. Reprinted in Reinhold Niebuhr, *Christian Realism and Political Problems,* New York, Scribner's, 1953, pp. 15-31.

FOREIGN TRADE, AID, AND INVESTMENT

[1] From a press release of October 1956, announcing the publication of a booklet, *Peace Is Positive,* by Haldore Hanson, published by the Union for Democratic Action Educational Fund, Inc.

[2] The three research agencies are Committee for Economic Development, a business-sponsored organization; Research Center in Economic Development and Cultural Change, University of Chicago; and Center for International Studies, Massachusetts Institute of Technology.

[3] *A New Emphasis on Economic Development Abroad,* International Advisory Board, Washington, D.C., March 4, 1957.

THE WAR OF WORDS AND IDEAS

[1] *Militant Liberty,* a pamphlet distributed by the Office of Admiral Arthur W. Radford, Chairman, Joint Chiefs of Staff, Washington 25, D.C., November 2, 1955, 13 pp. and 9 charts.

[2] See Frederick C. Barghoorn, *The Soviet Image of the United States:* New York, Harcourt, Brace and Co., 1950.

[3] *UNESCO Currier,* Paris, February 1957.

[4] *New York Times,* March 3, 1957, p. 10.

[5] "Words Are Not Enough," *The Nation,* March 13, 1943, p. 368.

⁶ *Departments of State, Justice, the Judiciary, and Related Agencies Appropriations, 1958.* Hearings before the Subcommittee of the Senate Appropriations Committee, 85th Congress, first session, Washington, D.C., 1957, page 1138.

⁷ See James Reston, "Let the Atomic Dust Settle," *New York Times,* June 2, 1957, page E 10.

⁸ This leaflet is reproduced and the incident about it recorded in *Truth Is Our Weapon,* by Edward W. Barrett: New York, Funk & Wagnalls Co., pp. 152-156.

⁹ *Highlights of the United States Information Agency Activities in Connection with the Hungarian Revolution,* reprinted in Congressional Record, Washington, D.C., March 18, 1957, pp. 3423-3424.

¹⁰ *Life,* May 19, 1952.

¹¹ "U. S. Information Program," *Department of State Bulletin,* July 18, 1948, pp. 88, 89. See also: George V. Allen, "Telling Our Side of the Story," *Department of State Bulletin,* January 30, 1949, pp. 142-143.

¹² *New York Times,* editorial, November 25, 1952.

¹³ *New York Times,* March 23, 1950.

¹⁴ *Washington Post,* March 26, 1950.

¹⁵ *New York Times,* November 23, 1950.

THE PUBLIC AND FOREIGN POLICY

¹ *The Public Philosophy,* Little, Brown & Co., Boston, 1955, pp. 20, 21.

² *In Defense of the National Interest,* Knopf, New York, 1951, p. 224.

³ "The Bases of a Foreign Program," *New York Times Magazine,* January 6, 1957, p. 11.

⁴ *Profiles in Courage,* Harper, New York, 1955, pp. 16, 17.

⁵ *Politics Among Nations,* Knopf, New York, 2nd ed., p. 135.

INDEX

INDEX

LIVING AGE BOOKS

Published by MERIDIAN BOOKS, INC.
17 Union Square West, New York 3, New York

LIVING AGE BOOKS, a vital series of inexpensive editions published by MERIDIAN BOOKS, INC., will contain works of proven merit on history, art, literature, theology, and Biblical studies, as they illuminate the development of Christian tradition in the West. Ask your bookseller for these handsome, well-made volumes.

Titles listed here are not necessarily available in the British Empire.

MERIDIAN BOOKS

17 Union Square West, New York 3, New York

FALL 1957

M46 POLITICS AND THE NOVEL *by Irving Howe*

M47 A SHORTER HISTORY OF SCIENCE *by William Cecil Dampier*

M48 A GUIDE TO CONTEMPORARY FRENCH LITERATURE *by Wallace Fowlie.* Meridian Original

M49 RENAISSANCE OF THE 12TH CENTURY *by C. H. Haskins*

M50 NEW POETS OF ENGLAND AND AMERICA *Edited and selected by Donald Hall, Robert Pack and Louis Simpson. Introduced by Robert Frost.* Meridian Original

M51 ST. AUGUSTINE *by M. C. D'Arcy*

MERIDIAN GIANT

MG9 THE LITERATURE OF THE SPANISH PEOPLE *by Gerald Brenan*

MG10 FILM FORM AND THE FILM SENSE *by Sergei Eisenstein*

MG11 LITERATURE IN AMERICA *Selected and introduced by Philip Rahv.* Meridian Original

MG12 THE DISSOCIATION OF A PERSONALITY *by Morton Prince*

MERIDIAN LIBRARY

ML5 EARLY GREEK PHILOSOPHY *by John Burnet*

ML6 PROLEGOMENA TO THE HISTORY OF ANCIENT ISRAEL *by Julius Wellhausen*

ML7 A GRAMMAR OF SCIENCE *by Karl Pearson Introduced by Ernest Nagel*

ML8 A HISTORY OF AESTHETIC *by Bernard Bosanquet*

GREENWICH EDITIONS

Original Clothbound Editions

ON ART AND LITERATURE: 1896–1919 *by Marcel Proust.*

ON LOVE: ASPECTS OF A SINGLE THEME *by José Ortega y Gasset.* Translated by Toby Talbot

GOD AND THE WAYS OF KNOWING *by Jean Danielou, S.J.*

Titles listed here are not necessarily available in the British Empire.